LEARN GUITAR FOR BEGINNERS

Published by:
Guitarschool
© Norman Gänser 2023
All rights reserved

Warmly welcome

This guitar school is the perfect introduction to the world of the guitar.
It teaches the most important basic knowledge about the "classical" method (fingerpicking, fingerstyle) in a modern, contemporary way.

When designing the courses consideration was given as to how the learning content could be conveyed in a very straightforward and comprehensible way, so as to make it possible for you to gain a solid training not only in this online self-study programme, but also as an accompaniment in face-to-face lessons with a teacher.

Norman Gänser

The learning material was developed with great care and conveys the basics such as, for example, the correct posture and technique.
The book is designed in gradual steps and thus creates the best conditions for successful playing, regardless of what kind of guitar you may play on later or which musical style you decide to pursue in the future.

 ## Audio and Video Files

1. Point your camera to the QR code.

2. The smartphone asks if you want to open the website.

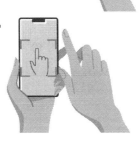

3. Learn guitar and have fun!

 https://www.guitarschool24.com/courses/guitar-book/

Contents

Textbook and Video Courses

© Norman Gänser
This edition:
© 2023 Verlag Guitarschool
Robert Hamerling Gasse 3, 1150 Vienna
norman@guitarschool.at
1. Auflage ISBN: 978-3-200-08562-6

Support and Cooperation
Didactics: Sigrid Kaiser, Armin Egger
Graphics: Sabrina Plesnik, Thomas Canori
Coverdesign: Wolkenart - Marie-Katharina Becker
Presentation of the pieces of music: Julia Renner, Kian Soofizadeh

---

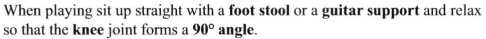

 1

When playing sit up straight with a **foot stool** or a **guitar support** and relax
so that the **knee** joint forms a **90° angle**.
Place your left foot on the stool and hold the guitar in both hands.
There are thus four points of contact:

(1) in your chest area

(2) on your right forearm

(3) on your left thigh

(4) on the inside of your right thigh

Finding the right position

☑ The guitar rests the main part of its **weight on your left thigh**.

☑ **The head** of the guitar is approximately **level with your ears.**

☑ Now you can adjust the correct **angle to your body**.
To do this sit up straight and **let the guitar fall onto your chest**.
It should now be leaning slightly towards you so that you can see
the strings and the fretboard.

☑ **Relax your right forearm onto the edge** of the guitar.
This will help you imagine a line from the bridge to the edge
which will enable you to find the right position for your forearm.

The right hand

Now you can place the **thumb** of your right hand on the lowest string,
your index finger, your middle finger, and your ring finger
on the three highest strings. From your view point the thumb
should be a little further left from the fingers.

Well done!

Miscellaneous

▶2 The Strings

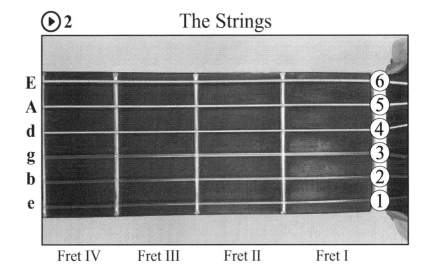

Fret IV   Fret III   Fret II   Fret I

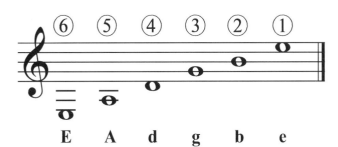

⑥ ⑤ ④ ③ ② ①

E   A   d   g   b   e

The strings of the guitar are indicated by numbers in circles!

Mnemonic: **E**lephants **A**nd **D**onkeys **G**row **B**ig **E**ars

---

Left Hand

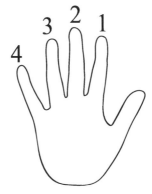

Right Hand

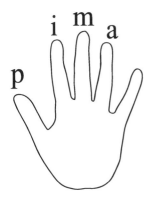

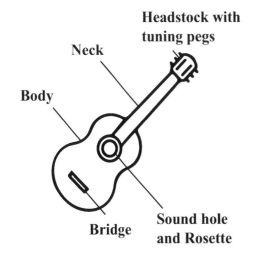

Headstock with tuning pegs

Neck

Body

Bridge

Sound hole and Rosette

1 = index finger
2 = middle finger
3 = ring finger
4 = little finger

p = thumb (pulgar)
i = index finger (indice)
m = middle finger (medio)
a = ring finger (anular)

The Thumb Pluck (p)

 3

With an **open thumb pluck** the thumb does not touch the lower strings when moving. The index, middle and ring fingers are placed on strings ③, ② and ①. They act as an **anchor**, providing stability and helping the thumb to **orientate** itself.

The edge of the thumb tip is placed on the string. While the **thumb plucks**, it remains **almost stretched.** The movement occurs in the vertebral joint (near the wrist) and resembles a **flat ellipse**. After the pluck it **'springs back' to its starting position** and again rests **on the string that is to be plucked next**.

Thumb **p** before the pluck on string ④
(initial position)

Thumb **p** after the pluck

Play the open strings with the thumb **p** in a regular rhythm.

Count:

1	2	3	4	1	2	3	4 ...								
④	④	④	④	⑤	⑤	⑤	⑤	⑥	⑥	⑥	⑥	⑤	⑤	⑤	⑤ :‖

1	2	3	1	2	3 ...						
⑤	⑤	⑤	④	④	④	⑤	⑤	⑤	⑥	⑥	⑥ :‖

⑥	⑥	⑥	⑥	⑤	⑤	⑤	⑤	④	④	④	④	⑤	⑤	⑤	⑤ :‖

The Stave

The **stave** consists of **five lines** and **four spaces**.
The lines and the spaces are **numbered from bottom to top**.

The first seven **letters of the alphabet** are used to name the notes:

c - d - e - f - g - a- h

The Treble Clef

The stave is also called the **G-Clef** because it begins on the 2nd line of the stave and indicates where the note G is to be found. All the notes now have a fixed position in the stave. The treble (or G-) clef is one of the most used clefs.

As the guitar sounds one octave (8 notes) lower than the notation, there may be an 8 under the treble clef.

You have space here to write the treble clef yourself.

❗ The clef thus determines the pitch of the notes in the stave.
• Now all that is missing is some information about the length of the notes (note values)

The Rest Stroke
(Apoyando)

4

In the case of the **rest stroke** (in short: Apoyando – in Spanish: apoyar = to support), the fingers remain on the adjacent string after the pluck.
The index finger **i** rests on its very tip on string ③. Then pressure is applied to the string in the direction of the top of the guitar until the string lies under the level of the other strings.

The index finger **plucks and stays on the adjacent string** above it.
At the same time the middle finger **m** is prepared and rests on its very tip on string ③.
The middle finger **m** now plucks the string. The movement looks as though the fingers are 'walking'.
The whole time the thumb **p** rests lightly on string ⑥ as support.

The index finger **i** before plucking string ③

The index finger **i** after the pluck

Try to play Apoyando with your index finger **i** on string ③

i　　　*i*　　　...
③　　　③　│　③　　　③　│　③　　　③　│　③　　　③　:‖

Play with your middle finger **m**:

m　　　*m*　　　...
③　　　③　│　③　　　③　│　③　　　③　│　③　　　③　:‖

Now play with your fingers **i** (index finger) and **m** (middle finger):

i　*m*　*i*　*m*　...
③ ③ ③ ③│③ ③ ③ ③│③ ③ ③ ③│③ ③ ③ ③:‖

Note and Rest Values

	Note Values		Rest Values	
Semibreve (o)	𝗈	=	▬	Semibreve rest = **4 Beats**
Minim (♩) (half note)	♩ ♩	=	▬ ▬	Minim rest = **2 Beats**
Crotchet (♩) (quarter note)	♩♩♩♩	=	𝄽𝄽𝄽𝄽	Crochet rest = **1 Beat**

The semibreve rest touches the line **above**, the minim rest lies **under** the line.
Mnemonic: The minim rest only rests a little while and lies down!

Time Signatures

The **time signature** can be found at the beginning of the piece of music. It consists of two digits one above the other.

 4
4 The upper digit shows the **number of beats** per bar.
The lower digit shows what **note value** a beat has.

A bar must always be filled completely with note or rest values!
Thus, in a **4/4** -time signature there must be 4 crochets in each bar.

Count out loud and clap:

In a **3/4** -time signature there are 3 crochets in each bar.

Count out loud and clap:

❗ **A dot behind the note extends this note by half its value.**
 • **Thus, for a note with three beats one adds a dot behind a minim.**

Lesson 1
The note g

We will start with the note **g.**
It can be found on string ③

The number in front of the note indicates the fingering.
'Finger 0' means Open String.

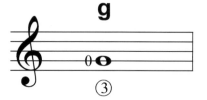

Open String **g**

▶ **5**   **Easy Going**

*Start with finger i (index finger) in the rest stroke.
When you get back to finger i, then you have done everything right!

▶ **6**   **Three in a Row**

The repeat sign

▶ **7**   **Marching String**

*The letters above the notes are chord symbols to accompany the tune. You do not need to play them!

Rhythmical Exercises

Play in rest strokes and count!
The metronome will set the beat.

A metronome is a mechanical or electronic device which specifies a constant tempo
through acoustical impulses at regular intervals.

© Norman Gänser
www.guitarschool24.com

Lesson 2
The note a

The note a can be found
on the 2nd fret on string ③

a is reached with the
middle finger (finger **2**).

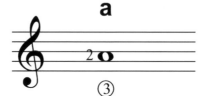

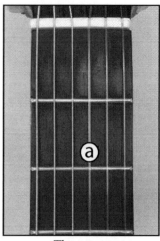

The note **a**

⏵11 Exercise

11.1   **11.2**

Repeat the bar sections.

⏵12 Soft Fret

Lightly grip in the **front third of the fret!
The fingertip should touch **as perpendicular as possible.**
The finger joints remain **angled and do not bend.**

⏵13 Counting Loud

**Let your 2nd finger rest until g is plucked.

Position of the Gripping Hand

Lightly place the **fingertip** (finger 2) in the front third of the fret, **before the metal bar!** The fingertip should be placed as perpendicular as possible, both **finger joints remaining angled** and not bent. The position of your hand should thus be **as natural as possible**.
The other fingers hover **relaxed** above the fretboard.

The fingers for note **a**

The thumb is on the back of the neck of the guitar **opposite** the fingers. Its **basic position** is **between the index and the middle fingers**. It is always **mobile** and only exercises **light** counter pressure.
The thumb lies **flat** and remains **stretched** rather than angled!

The light "counter pressure" comes from the base joint (near the wrist).
The **weight of the arm helps** when you press down on the strings and so relieves the thumb!

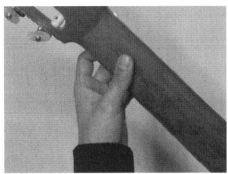

The thumb for note **a**

Finger Exercise

4-Finger-Grip: Lay all four fingers on string ③. Start with the index finger (finger **1**) on fret **V**, finger **2** rests on fret **VI**, finger **3** on fret **VII** and finger **4** on fret **VIII.**

Now lift finger 1 up and let it fall again on the string.
Repeat the movement four times. While doing this keep the other fingers relaxed in their position.
The fingertips should be touching almost perpendicularly.
Now do the exercise with finger **2**, then finger **3** and finger **4** as well.

The „**4-finger-grip**" is a proven coordination and stretching exercise for the fingers.
It also helps us to find the correct position for the thumb.

Illustrating the hand position with a pencil.
In contrast to the gripping fingers, where the fingertips rest at an angle, the thumb is outstretched. The pressure point is somewhere above the front joint.

Rhythmical Exercises

Play in rest strokes and count!
The metronome will set the beat.

Lesson 3
The note b

The note **b** can be found on the 2nd open string.

On the musical stave the note **b** sits on the **middle line.**
*Above the middle line, in monodic notation, the neck of the note goes downwards to the left of the head.

middle line ——>

Open String **b**

▶17 **Exercise**

Alternate your Fingers i and m always, even when changing strings!

17.1   m   i   m   i   m   i   17.2   i   m   i   m   i   m

17.3   m   i   m   i   m   i
       i   m   i   m   i   m

*Try beginning with the middle finger.

17.4   m   a   m   a   m   a   m   a
       i   m   i   m   i   m   i   m

*Also play the exercises with the middle finger **m** and ring finger **a.**

▶18 **Going Down**

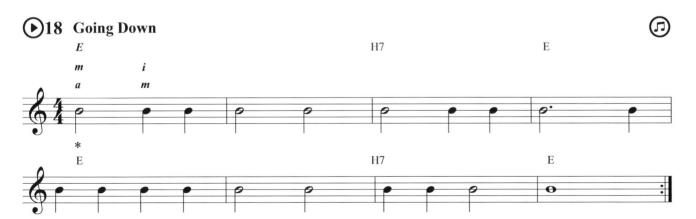

*

© Norman Gänser   15
www.guitarschool24.com

19 Rocking Strings

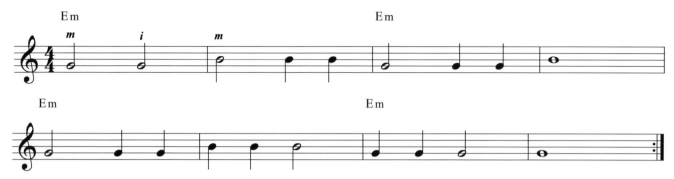

20 Little Melody

*Leave finger 2 resting until the note b is sounded.

21 Choral

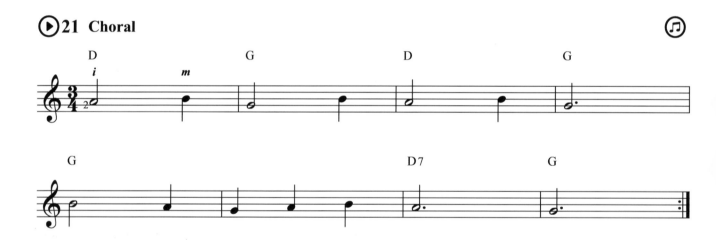

Number and name the strings and the frets:

Fret ___   Fret ___   Fret ___

Lesson 4
The note c

The note **c** is to be found on the first fret on the 2nd string.

c is played with the index finger 1.

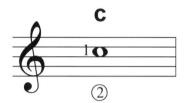

The note **c**

▶22 Exercise

22.1

22.2

*Start with **a**. The thumb and the hand position do not change.

▶23 Desert Song

$$\overset{*}{\mathbf{C}} = \frac{4}{4}$$

The letter **C** is used here as the note signature.
The **C** behind the clef means $\frac{4}{4}$ beat.

The note **d** can be found on the 3rd fret
on the 2nd string.

d is played with the ringer finger 3,
or with the little finger 4!

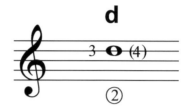

The note **d**

▶ 24 Exercise

24.1

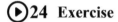

*The dashed line means that you should let your finger rest (here finger 1).

24.2

**Start with placing finger 3 and finger 1 together!

▶ 25 Team Work

▶ 26 Changing Moods

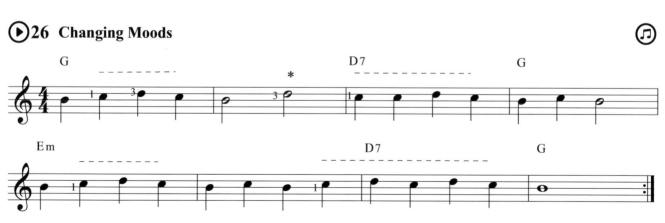

The First Five Notes
of the G-Major Scale

27 G-Major

28 Lullaby Trad.

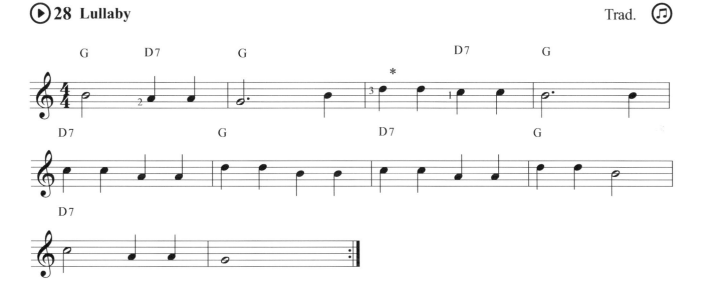

Write any tune that you like with the notes that you know and play it on your guitar.
Do not forget the time signature!

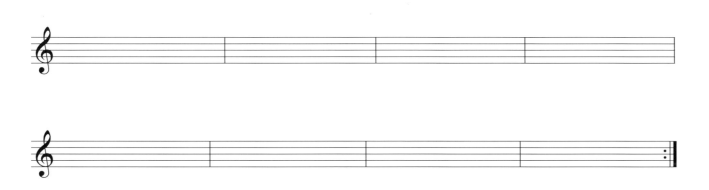

Lesson 5
The note e

The note **e** can be
found on the open string ① .

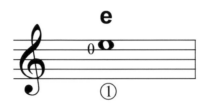

open string **e**

▶29 **Exercise**

29.1

29.2

*Play three notes per string. Take care to always pluck even when changing strings.

If there is not supposed to be a sound, there will be a **rest sign.**
In the next exercise try to mute the note that you have just played with the next
finger by laying it on the string. Then play the next note with the same finger.

29.3

30 The Young Bride

Adapted from Béla Bartók (1881–1945)

31 Matrjoschka

Russian

Lesson 6
The note f

The note **f** can be found on the first fret on the 1st string.

f is played with the index finger **1**!

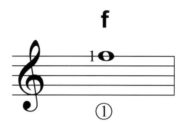

The note **f**

▶ **32   Mystical Song**

*Start with **d** and leave finger **3** resting until the **f** sounds.

The note g

The note **g** is to be found on the third fret of the 1st string.

g is played with the ring finger **3**, or with the little finger **4**!

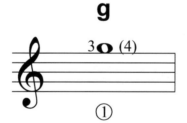

The note **g**

▶ **33   C- Major Scale (first 5 notes)**

▶ 34 On the Edge

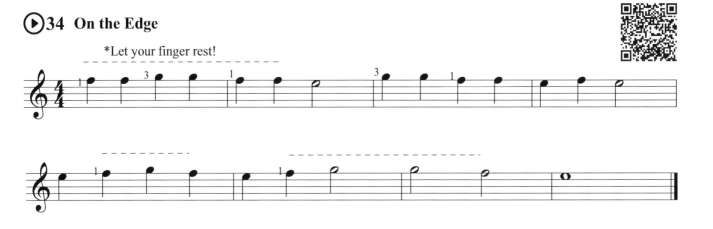

*Let your finger rest!

▶ 35 Shadow Groove

Trad.

The Upbeat

The upbeat begins before the first accentuated beat 1.
It is an incomplete bar that stands at the beginning
of a tune and it forms a complete bar with the last bar.

The count in is:

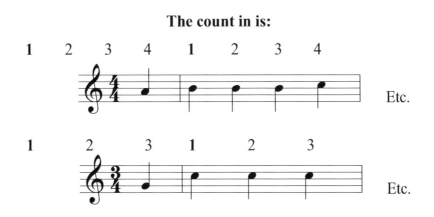

1 2 3 4 1 2 3 4

Etc.

1 2 3 1 2 3

Etc.

▶36 La Ibera

Norman Gänser

*The rest values are always counted together.

▶37 Gstanzl

Traditional Alpine Song

▶38 The Rooftop

Norman Gänser

Lesson 7
The note d

The note **d** can be found
on the open string ④

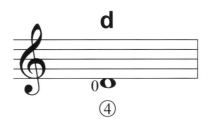

Open String **d**

▶ 39 Pump d String

*Put **i**, **m**, **a** on strings **3**, **2**, and **1**!

▶ 40 Ladder

▶ 41 Country Walz

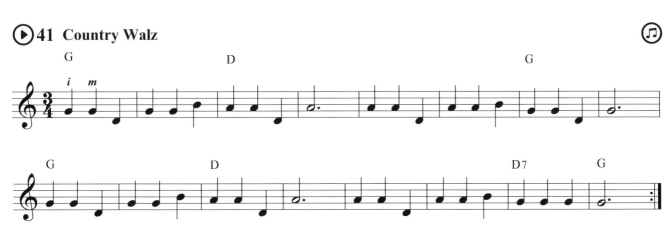

The Quaver

Two quavers are played on one **crotchet beat**.
You can recognise them by the **little flag** on the neck.

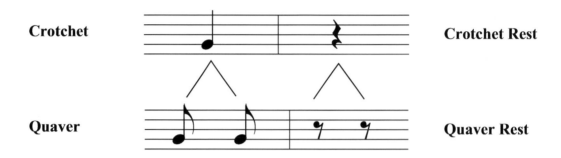

Crotchet		Crotchet Rest
Quaver		Quaver Rest

▶ **42 Exercise**

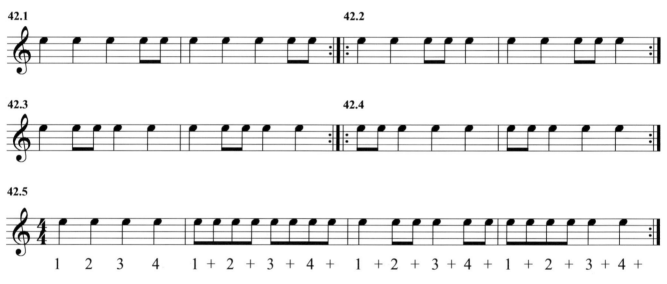

42.1

42.2

42.3

42.4

42.5

1 2 3 4   1 + 2 + 3 + 4 +   1 + 2 + 3 + 4 +   1 + 2 + 3 + 4 +

*Quavers are joined by a bar if they are written next to each other.

▶ **43 Eastern Melody**

The $\frac{2}{4}$ Time Signature

The $\frac{2}{4}$ time signature has a heavy and a light beat. **1 2 1 2 1 2 1 2** ...

EIt is therefore more static than the $\frac{4}{4}$ beat in which the 1 is more accentuated than the 3 (see Time Signatures Characteristics).

Time Signature Characteristics

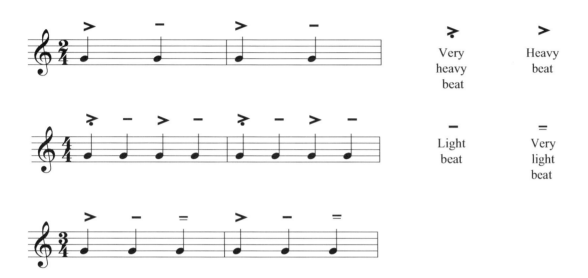

▶ **44 Merily We Roll Along**   American 🎵

Lesson 8
The note A

The note **A** can be found
on the open string ⑤

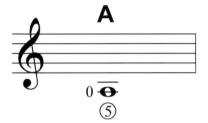

A

Open String **A**

▶45 Walking Bass

Der Ton E

The note **E** can be found
on the open string ⑥

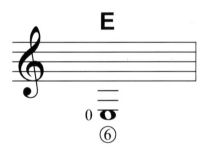

E

Open String **E**

▶46 Adé Adé

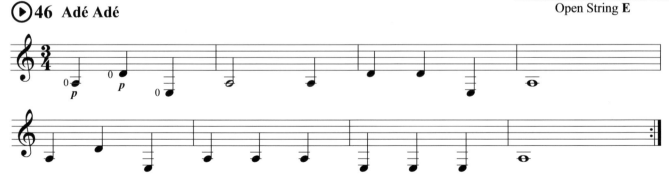

Accompanying a song with open strings

Until now we have got to know that guitar as a **monophonic instrument**.
For centuries, the guitar counted as one of the most popular instruments for
accompanying songs. In the next piece the tune is accompanied by **open strings**.
Please **pay attention to your fellow players** as well if you are in a group!

47 Arabian Dance

Norman Gänser

48 Bazar

First play Guitar 1 and then Guitar 2

Norman Gänser

Exercise Section

Finger Exercise

If a d follows a g, or vice versa, the notes are played with fingers **3** and **4**.
A free finger therefore serves as a 'spare finger' to join the sounds.
Make sure you place your fingers precisely in the drill.

▶49 Farmer´s March

Folk song around 1905

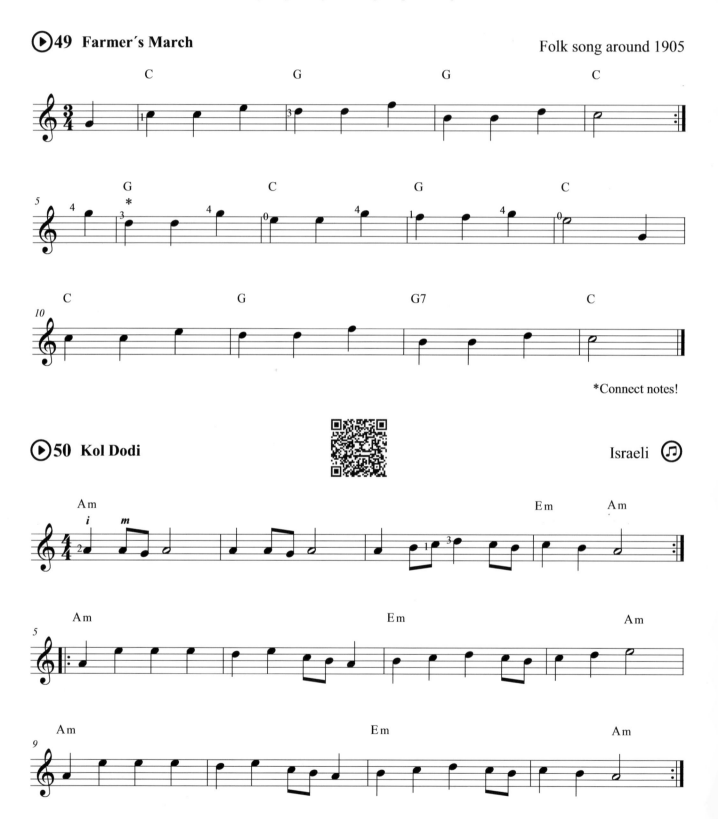

*Connect notes!

▶50 Kol Dodi

Israeli

© Norman Gänser
www.guitarschool24.com

▶51 Ja Nus Hon Pris   Adapted from Richard the Lionheart (1157–1199) 🎵

▶52 Running Fingers   Norman Gänser

53 **Rumba Flamenca**

Norman Gänser

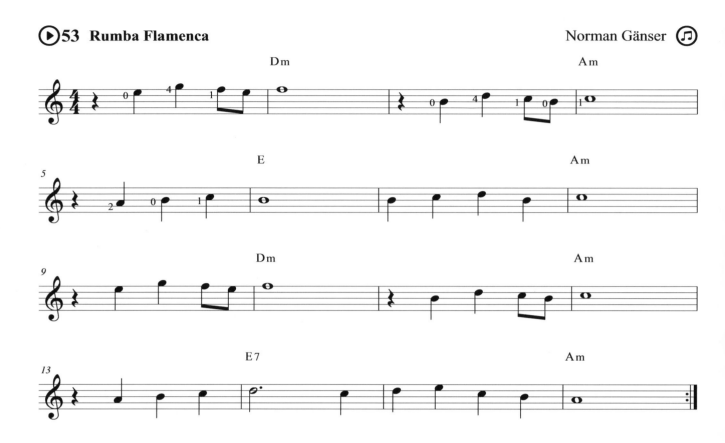

Congratulations

You have successfully completed
the Elementary Level 1!

Chords

If three different notes are played at the same time we speak of a **chord or a triad**.
Chords are mainly used as accompaniment for tunes or songs.

We therefore need only three strings to be able to play a chord (small chords).
Alternate between the following chords on the descant strings ①, ② and ③.

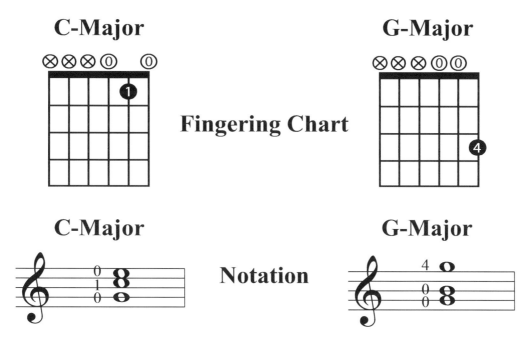

C-Major   **Fingering Chart**   **G-Major**

C-Major   **Notation**   **G-Major**

* Grip the c as usual with finger **1**.

If the notes are one above the other, then they are played **at the same time.

Strumming

Place your thumb on the d string (String ④) and strum the strings with your fingers (i, m, a)
by slightly opening your hand. It is the index finger i which above all touches the strings.
You can also strum upwards by using the fingertip and/or the edge of your nail.
Count, for example, 1 + 2 + 3 + 4 + ...

Strumming with the nail surface.

Strumming with the fingertip and/or nail edge.

Small Chords

These **three-part chords** (triads) are played on strings ①, ② and ③.

C-Major
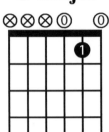

G-Major
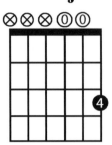

G7
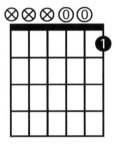

E-Minor
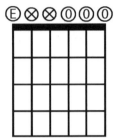

E-Major
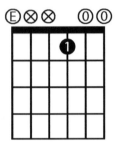

E7
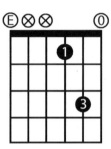

A-Major
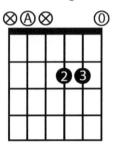

A-Minor
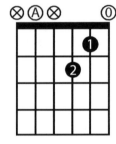

D-Major
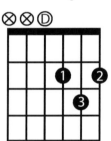

D7
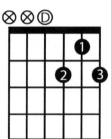

D-Minor
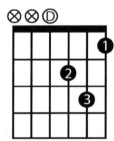

F-Major
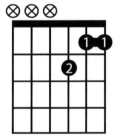

B-Major
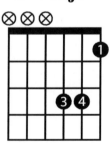

H-Major
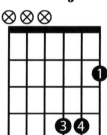

H7
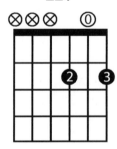

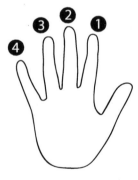

Examples of appropriate chord progressions:
C-Major – G – G7 – C-Major
A-Minor - C-Major- G-Major - E-Major
A-Major - D-Major - E-Major - A-Major
D-Major - A-Major - G-Major - D-Major ...

⓪ Open String

⊗ Does not sound

Ⓔ Ⓐ Ⓓ Bass strings
(are not played here)

Discover your own chord progressions or accompany the tunes in the book!
More 5- or 6-part chords can be found in **"Online Elementary Guitar 2"**.

Free Stroke
(Tirando)

The following exercises are played in **Free Stroke** or Tirando (from the Spanish word tirar = to pull). The fingers do **not** touch the adjacent string after the stroke.

The fingers move away just above the adjacent string, in the direction of the hand palm. The movement of the individual fingers is similar to when we form a fist. So, imagine you are making a fist (see illustration) but only with one finger.

Avoid "plucking" the string away and upwards from the soundboard!

We start in the basic position: index-, middle and ring fingers on the strings ③, ② and ①. The thumb rests on string ④.

Basic Position

Index finger i after the strum

▶ 55 Exercise

Play the g-string several times in succession with the **index finger i**.

Take care to ensure that the plucking finger does not touch any other string!

The thumb, index finger and ring finger rest as relaxed as possible on the strings.
When you are familiar with the movement, play the b-string several times with the **middle finger m**.
The other fingers again rest on the strings.

Now the **ring finger a**. Consciously relax your fingers and hand after every stroke. The fingers thereby return to their starting position.

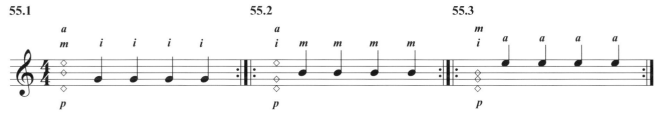

*The "fixed" fingers are represented in the notation by open, rhombic notes.

In this exercise the thumb and one finger respectively take it in turns to play.

The notes should all sound together! The fixed or "constrained" fingers rest loosely on the strings.

This technique provides stability in the plucking hand and prevents the fingers dropping onto the soundboard!

55.4

55.5

55.6

▶ 56

Celtic Tune

Norman Gänser

Apoyando

* **Tirando**

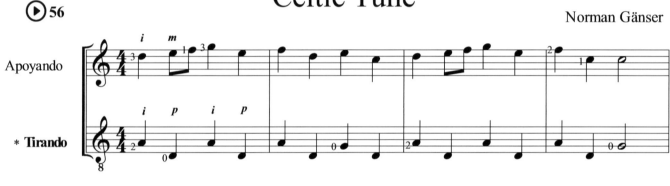

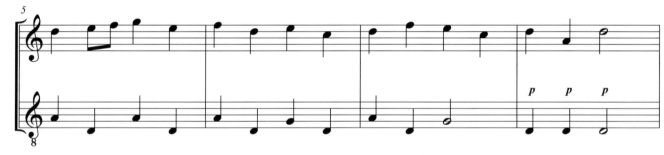

*First play the 2nd part (Tirando) and then the 1st part (Apoyando)

Arpeggios

In an **arpeggio** the individual notes are "plucked" one after another in **Free Stroke** (Tirando). In this way one can let several notes sound together on different strings, without having to instantly mute them again (Arpeggio).

▶ **57 Arpeggio-Exercise**

☑ Place your fingers in the **basic position** again on the strings.

☑ Now pluck the strings one after another without muting them again! First the thumb **p**, then the index finger **i**, middle finger **m**, and lastly the ring finger **a**.

☑ After the ring finger **a**, prepare the thumb **p** to strum once again.

☑ After strumming with the thumb at the beginning of the beat, we again place all fingers on the strings ①, ② and ③ **(Basic Position)**.

☑ All the notes sound together, until the end of the beat even though they are written as crochets.

Arpeggio-Exercise 57.1

Arpeggio-Exercise 57.2

Two- Part Notation:

If the bass notes continue to sound while other notes are played, we need two parts for this. In order to be able to distinguish better between the two parts, the bass notes have a downward stem, the melody notes have an upward stem!

Melody Part

Bass Part

Lesson 9
The note e

The note e can be found on the 2nd fret bar on string ④ and is played with the middle finger (Finger 2).

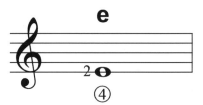

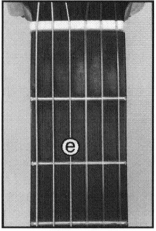

The note **e**

▶ **58 Exercise**

Try to lay Finger 2 on the string with no pressure.

Now slowly and alternately pluck the string. The sound will be muffled. Now slowly increase the pressure until the **e** sounds. You will notice how little pressure is actually needed for this.

Pressure Curve

The note f

Note f can be found on the 3rd fret bar on string ④ and is played with the ring finger (Finger 3).

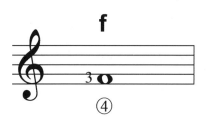

The note **f**

58.1

*While you play f, let your finger lie on e until d is plucked! There should be no break of sound between the notes!

Dynamics

In order to be able to make a piece of music more interesting, there are musical notations in the scores. They describe properties such as volume, tempo, and character, which the music is supposed to have.

p   (piano) = soft   crescendo = becoming louder

f   (forte) = loud   decrescendo = becoming softer

▶ 59 **Exercise**

Volume Curve

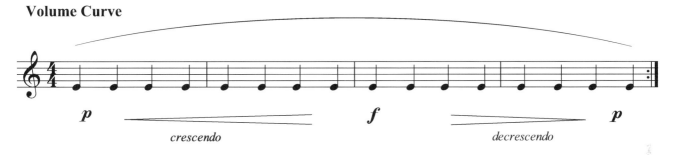

▶ 60

Tirandos

Norman Gänser

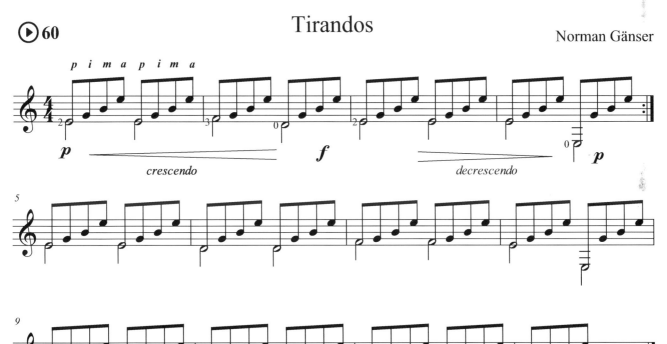

Also play the piece with other plucking patterns.

Lesson 10
The note C₁

The note C1 can be found on the
3rd fret bar on string ⑤ .

C$_{(1)}$

The note **C**

It is played with the ring
finger (Finger 3).

▶ **61 Exercise**

The Tie

The tie joins two consecutive notes of the same pitch together.
The second note joined by the tie does **not** have to be plucked again!
The first note simply continues to sound. The values of both notes are counted together.

The tie is also used to let a note sound **over a bar line!**

Morning Has Broken

▶ **62**

From England

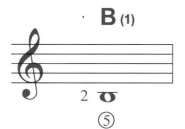

The note **B** can be found on the
2nd fret bar on string ⑤.
Note B is played with the index
finger (Finger 2).

The Note B

The Close Chord Strum

If the notes are one above the other, they are played **simultaneously**.
The joint strum of **i, m and a** is no different from a strum with a single finger.
The fingers move at the same time (close), just above the adjacent strings.
Take care to strum the fingers at the same time and that every note in the chord sounds.

E-Moll

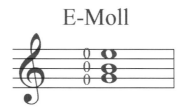

▶ **63 Exercise**

Play the chord with your index-, middle- and ring fingers.
Rest your thumb **p** first on the bass string E (string ⑥).

63.1

Now play with your thumb p and the close position strum with your fingers alternately.
When you play with your thumb, place your fingers again on the melody strings.
While the fingers are playing, the thumb is placed on the bass string (in preparation).

63.2

*Accompany the song "Alternate Strings" (Lesson 3).

Polka

Folk Dance

* On the first time through, the part in bracket 1 is played. After repeating from the beginning, on the second time through, bracket 1 is skipped, and bracket 2 is played immediately.

The so-called House Brackets are named **Prima-Volta** (the first time) and **Seconda-Volta** (the second time).

With Ease

▶ 65

Norman Gänser

Theme

p i m i p i m i

tirando

Variation 1

p i m i p i m i

Variation 2

a m i *a m i*

p *p*

Chords

Strumming Techniques

Basic Chords are those that occur the most often in the "First Position".
They are used to accompany songs. As such, they can be "plucked" or strummed.

Downstroke: To downstroke a chord, you use, as already discussed for the small chords, the back of the fingernail. Lift your hand until it hovers over the low E-string and simply let it drop. Now strum all the strings in one movement from the low E-string to the high E-string. The stroke should come from the wrist.

Upstroke: The upstroke is carried out with the back of the thumb fingernail. The wrist "turns" back until the hand is once again in the starting position. While strumming, all the strings do not have to be played.

Rhythmical Notation

The rhythmical notation indicates how often and in which direction the chords should be strummed. The symbols have the same value and the respective note values.

$$\diamondsuit = o \qquad \diamondsuit = \rho \qquad \int = \rho \qquad \int = \rho$$

The **strum direction** is indicated by the following symbols and arrows.

The downstroke ⊓ or ↑ (from the lowest to the highest string)
The upstroke V or ↓ (from the highest to the lowest string)

Downbeats 1 2 3 4 = Downstroke

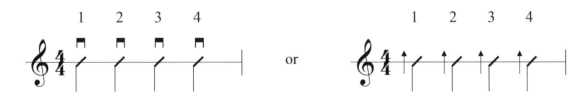

Upbeats + = Upstroke

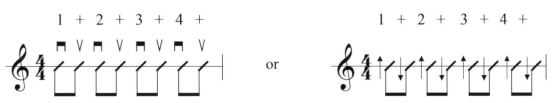

*On some tab- and note-platforms on the web, the arrows are drawn the other way around.
The same applies here: downbeats = downstrokes, upbeats (+) = upstrokes!

Fingering chart for E-Minor.
E-Minor is played with Finger 1
and Finger 2 simultaneously.

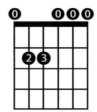

▶ **Exercise**

Volume Curve

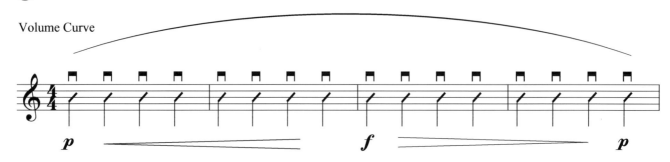

▶ 67

The Viking

Norman Gänser

Lesson 11
String ⑥

String ⑥ has the same note name as string ①!

The note **F** can be found on the 2nd fret bar on string ⑥ and is played with the index finger (Finger 1)!

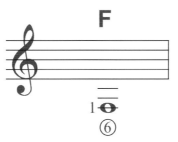

The note **G** can be found on the 3rd fret bar on the string ⑥ and is played with the ring finger (Finger 3).

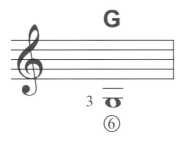

▶ Exercise

*Start in the Basic Position.
The thumb does not touch while playing (tirando).

**Now place your thumb on string ⑤
Index- and middle fingers play apoyando.

*ritardando

Sunrise

▶ 68

Norman Gänser

tirando

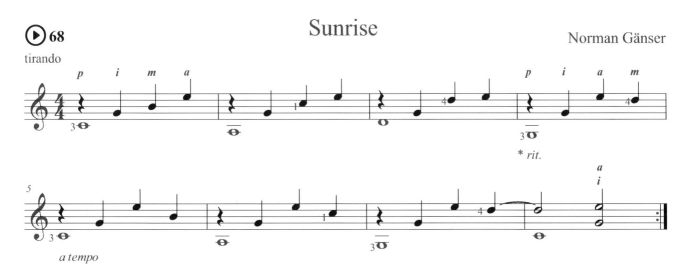

* rit.

a tempo

rit. is the abbreviation for ritardando and means becoming slower!
a tempo (italian for "at the previous or original tempo") cancels the preceding tempo change.

Accidentals
The Sharp ♯

The sharp ♯ is an accidental. It raises the note which follows it by half a tone (a semitone).
On the guitar the note is played one fret bar higher! The word "sharp" is added after the note name:

c sharp - d sharp - e sharp - f sharp - g sharp- a sharp - b sharp

Example **f sharp**:
f becomes f sharp
(one fret bar higher)

Accidentals apply for one bar!
Example c sharp:

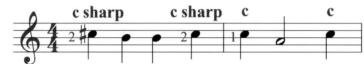

	f sharp	f sharp	c sharp	C sharp	g sharp	G sharp	d sharp	d sharp
String	①	④	②	⑤	③	⑥	②	④
Fret	2	4	2	4	1	4	4	1

Greensleeves

▶ 69

Trad. England

apoyando

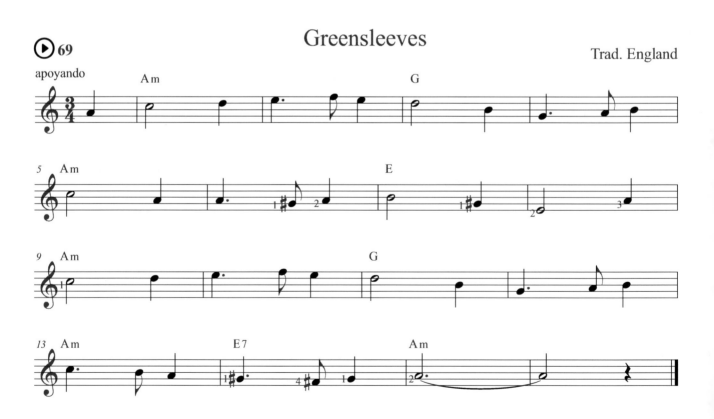

The ♭ Accidental

The ♭ accidental lowers the note that follows it by half a tone (a semitone).
On the guitar the note is played one fret bar lower!
The word 'flat' is added to the note name:

c flat - d flat - e flat - f flat - g flat - a flat - b flat

Example **b and es:**
b becomes b flat
e becomes e flat
(one fret bar lower)

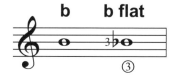

	b flat	b flat	e flat	e flat	a flat	A flat	d flat	d flat
String	③	⑤	②	④	③	⑥	②	⑤
Fret	3	1	4	1	1	4	2	4

▶ **70**

apoyando

Downtown Blues

Norman Gänser

The Natural ♮ Accidental

The natural symbol cancels out the sharp ♯ or the flat ♭ again.
It always applies within one bar!

47

Lesson 12

The Key Signature

The **C-Major** scale does **not have a key signature**!
Every **major** scale consists of **two half tone increments** and **five whole tone increments**.
The two natural half tone increments lie between **e and f** (third and fourth note in C-Major),
and between **b and c** (seventh and eighth note in C-Major).

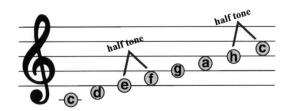

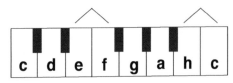

*Natural half tone increments on the piano keyboard

The distance from fret bar to fret bar is, in each case, a half tone increment!
Half tone increments = the distance between one fret bar
Whole tone increments = the distance between two fret bars

C-Major Scale

The G-Major Scale with Key Signature

If we play the major scale starting with the **note g**, the two half tone increments
have to again lie between the **third and fourth** notes and between the **seventh and eighth** notes.
Therefore, the **f is also raised a half tone** by the sharp **(f-sharp)**.

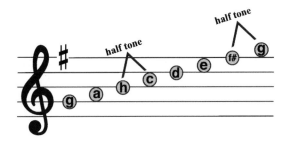

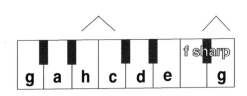

If the sharp sign is at the beginning of the piece, between the clef and the time signature,
it is called a **Key Signature**. This key signature applies for the **whole piece** and raises all notes
with the same name (all octaves)! **The G-Major scale has one sharp (f-sharp).**

G-Major Scale

The semiquavers are half as long as the quavers!

Count: 1 e + e 2 e + e 3 e + e 4 e + e ...

Air

Orchestersuite Nr. 3, BWV 1068

J.S. Bach 1685-1750

▶ 73

Bourree

J.S. Bach 1685-1750

▶ 74

Lesson 13
The offset strum with the thumb

The offset strum with the thumb makes it possible for you to accompany yourself when playing a melody. Play your index- and middle fingers in an alternating rest stroke (apoyando).One finger is thus always lying relaxed on the adjacent string and ensures stability. The thumb plays a **free stroke** (tirando).

▶ **75 Exercise**

▶ **76 Conversation**

Norman Gänser

This practice piece with empty bass strings is written in simplified "Guitar Notation".
The crochets in the bass simply continue to sound!

⏵ **78**

Light Walz

Norman Gänser

* > Accentuated Beat
The waltz is an Austrian dance in ¾ time with particular accentuation on the first beat!

The Offset Thumb Strum
with Bass Notes

In the following practice pieces the offset thumb strum is used with bass notes! Make sure that
the bass notes sound long enough! Leave your finger on the string according to the length of the note
while the other finger plays the tune! Play your index- and middle fingers in an alternating
rest stroke (apoyando). The thumb plays a free stroke (tirando).

79 Lazy Fingers

Trombone

Norman Gänser

Lesson 14
The simultaneous strum with the thumb

When simultaneously strumming with the thumb, we play with the index- and middle-fingers in an alternating rest stroke (apoyando). The thumb plays a free stroke (tirando). Make sure that the simultaneous strum by the fingers with the thumb is the same as the strum by the fingers without the thumb!

▶ **81 Exercise**

▶ **82 Unter den Linden**   Walther von der Vogelweide (1170 - 1230)

Dance

Sigrid Kaiser

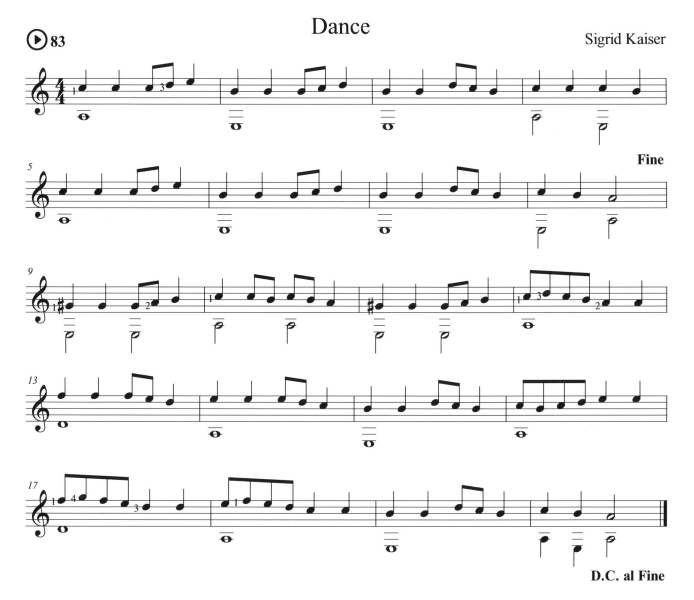

Fine

D.C. al Fine

D.C. = **Da Capo** (from the start) means that you should play from the beginning again.
You often find this playing instruction in conjunction with "al Fine" (to the end).
You thus play again from the start up to the symbol Fine.

Caesar

Norman Gänser

The Simultaneous Strum with Bass Notes

Index- and middle- fingers play alternating rest strokes, the thumb plays free strokes.
Let the bass notes sound as long as possible.

Four Seasons

A. Vivaldi (1687-1741)

Bella Bimba

From Italy

Sight-Reading is playing a piece that you have never seen before.
The following tips show you what you must look out for and help you to continue to improve.

1. Look closely at the time signature and count at least one bar in your head.
2. Are there any accidentals or natural accidentals?
2. Keep an eye on the melodic pattern, on movements, on note repetitions or note jumps.
3. Just as when you read a book, try to always read a little ahead.
4. Play at an appropriate, slow speed!

▶ 87

Ostinato

Norman Gänser

This practice exercise with bass notes is simply notated (the bass continues to sound).
The crochets just continue to sound! Initially there is also no fingering.

Lesson 15

E-Major

Fingering chart E-Major.
The E-Major chord is played
with three fingers.

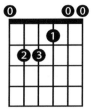

A-Minor

Fingering chart A-Minor.

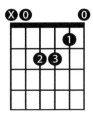

Milonga

► 88

Norman Gänser

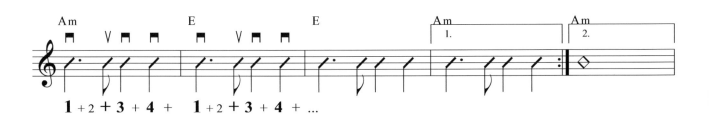

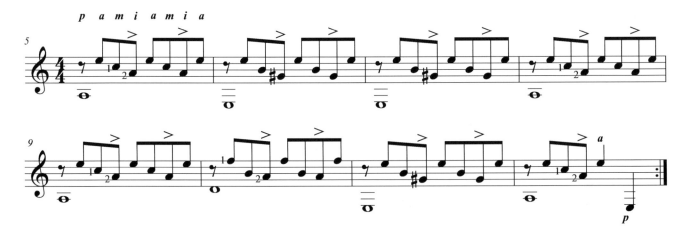

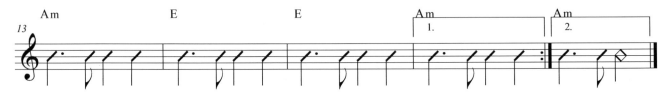

Asturias

Leyenda (Theme)

Adapted from Isaac Albeniz (1860-1909)

crescendo

diminuendo

* The **Fermata** is a musical articulating symbol and means that the note or pause can be held longer than the written note value, according to the player's wishes.

diminuendo = *decrescendo* and means "becoming softer"
crescendo = "becoming louder"

Malagueña

Adaptation: N.G.

Trad. from Spain

* *accelerando*

{ = Arpeggiated or broken chord!
The notes are strummed quickly and one after another.

accelerando means "increasing in speed".
Begin quite slowly and get a little faster.

Lesson 16
The note a

The note a can be found on
the 5th fret bar on string ①
and is played with the
little finger (Finger 4)!

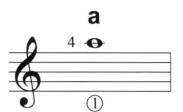

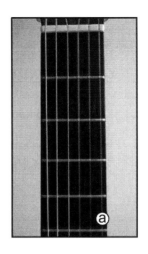

Korobeiniki
Console Theme

(Trad. Asian)

Pop Goes The Weasel

From Great Britain

Etude

Dionisio Aguado 1784-1849

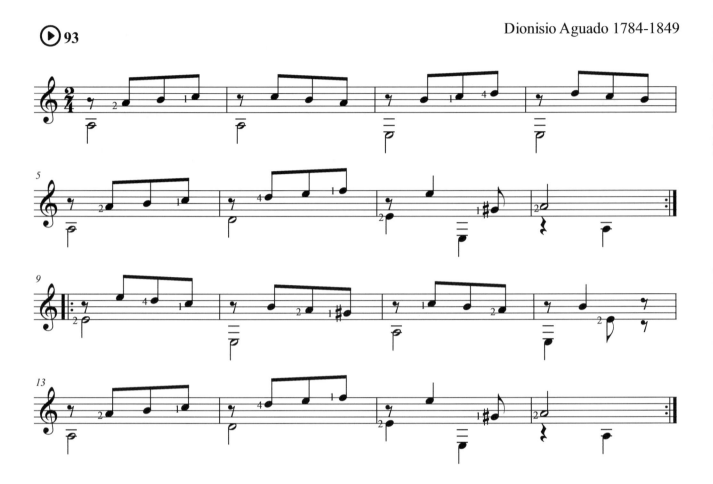

Congratulations

You have successfully
completed Part Two!

The most common chords

C-Major
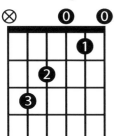

C7
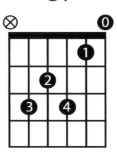

G-Major
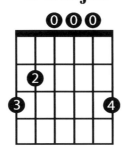

G7
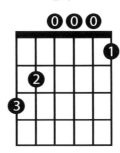

E-Minor
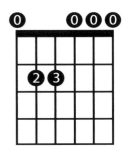

E-Major
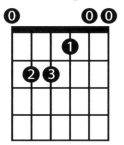

C7
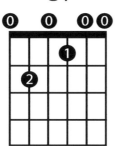

A-Major
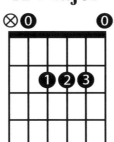

A7
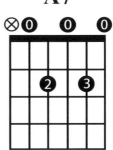

A-Minor
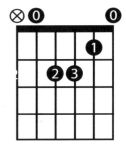

D-Major
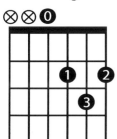

D7
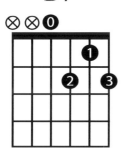

D-Minor
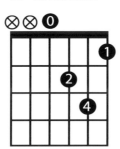

F-Major
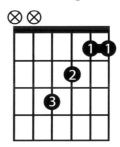

Fmaj7
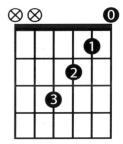

Bb-Major
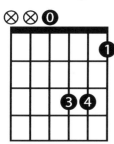

B-Major
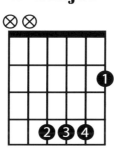

B7
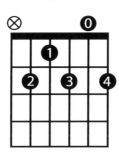

B-Minor
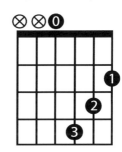

B-Minor7
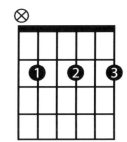

The Tabulator

The tabulator, tabs for short, is a graphic way of presenting the notes on a guitar.
The horizontal lines on the tabulator represent the six strings on the guitar.
The numbers on them indicate the fret bar on which you should press the strings.
Do not confuse these numbers with the fingering.

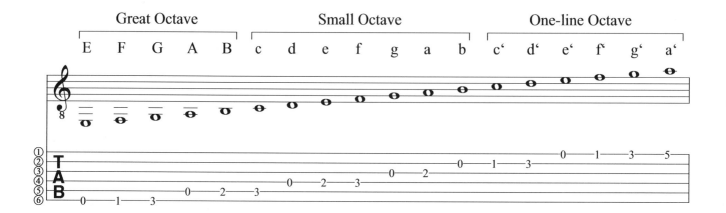

Arpeggios represented as tabs
The notes are played one after the other.

Arpeggios represented as tabs
The notes are played one after the other.

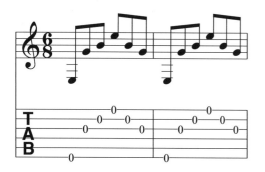

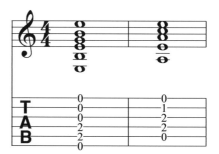

Although tabs show the sequence of the notes that are to be played, the tabulator alone does not reveal anything about the actual rhythm. Likewise, it does not show the fingering for either the right or the left hands. This makes it very difficult to learn a piece from a tabulator, particularly when one has never heard it before.
Classic notation clearly has an advantage here!

Arpeggios with simultaneous strum

The following piece is played **tirando** with the thumb and the fingers.
It is intended to introduce you to the wonderful guitar literature of the great masters.
Look out for the dynamic indications and arrange it in a musical way.

Andantino

Matteo Carcassi 1792 - 1853

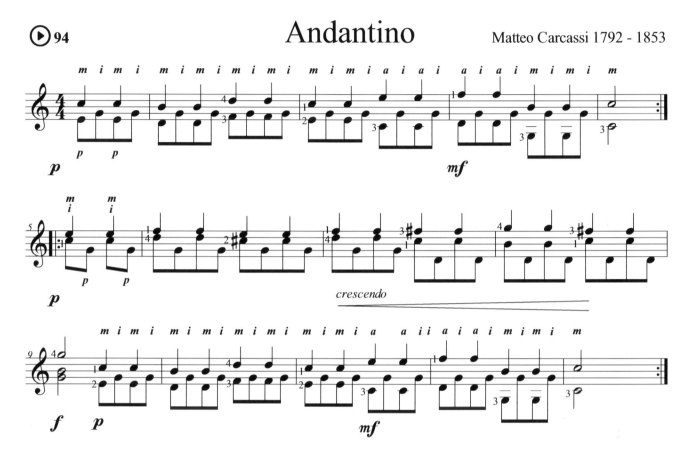

Tempo Markings

Overview of the most important tempo markings taken from Italian. Nowadays the tempo is indicated with a metronome rate, for example. ♩ = **60 bpm (Beats per minute)**

Largo	broad, slow	40-50 bpm
Grave	heavy	40-50 bpm
Lento	slow	50-60 bpm
Adagio	slow, calm	50-60 bpm
Andante	at a walking pace	60-80 bpm
Andantino	slightly faster than Andante	70-80 bpm
Moderato	moderate in pace	90-100 bpm
Allegretto	slightly slower than Allegro	100-120 bpm
Allegro	fast, quick, bright	120-140 bpm
Vivace, vivo	brisk, lively	150-180 bpm
Presto	fast	170-200 bpm
Prestissimo	very fast	>200 bpm

Tempo Change

Musical terms that indicate the tempo is changing!

The tempo increases:

accelerando (accel.) _____ becoming faster
stringendo (string.) _____ urgent
piu mosso _____ animated
piu vivo _____ lively

Related to the tempo:

rubato _____ flexible tempo
senza tempo _____ without time
poco a poco _____ little by little
subito ... _____ suddenly

The tempo decreases:

ritardando (rit.) _____ becoming slower
rallentando (rall.) _____ becoming slower
ritenuto _____ suddenly slower
meno mosso _____ less animated

Dynamics

Musical terms indicating volume!

pp _____ **pianissimo** _____ very soft
p _____ **piano** _____ soft
mp _____ **mezzopiano** _____ moderately soft
mf _____ **mezzoforte** _____ moderately loud
f _____ **forte** _____ loud
ff _____ **fortissimo** _____ very loud
fp _____ **fortepiano** _____ loud and immediately soft
sf _____ **sforzato** _____ with particular emphasis
crescendo (cresc.) $<$ _____ becoming louder
decrescendo (decresc.) $>$ _____ becoming softer
diminuendo (dim.) _____ becoming softer, diminishing

Articulating Symbols

Indications about the sound production.

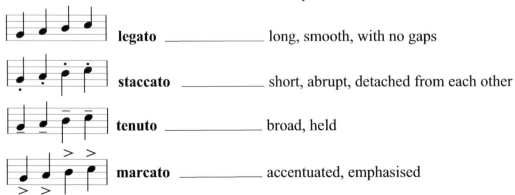

legato _____ long, smooth, with no gaps

staccato _____ short, abrupt, detached from each other

tenuto _____ broad, held

marcato _____ accentuated, emphasised

66
© Norman Gänser
www.guitarschool24.com

Tirando / Apoyando

Tirando is used for music passages where several strings must sound together. This applies to both arpeggios (a favourite composition technique for the classical guitar) and to polyphonic playing on several strings. The result is a "harp like" effect, which is simply not possible with the apoyando technique, as the adjacent string is muted. Thus, tirando can, in contrast to **apoyando**, be used for almost every passage. The tone of both techniques should however not differ.

Tirando-Exercise (Legato)

When playing with the nails (see Page 89), the **point of contact** with the string is exactly between the fingertip and the nail. Find and get a feeling for your point of contact by exerting some pressure on the string with *i*. How does it feel? Now let the string slide across the nail and play the free stroke tirando. Repeat the steps with finger *m* and play alternately. Play in 3/4- and 4/4-time signatures (almost) without a break in the sound!

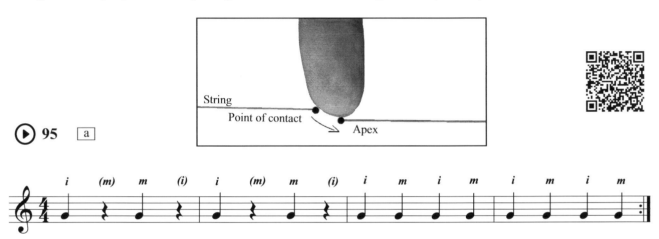

The **point of contact** of the finger and the nail and/or the fingertip should always be the same. To avoid the nails making a noise, the **fingertip** hits the string **a little earlier**.

[b] Make sure that the **legato** is clean (there should be no breaks in the sound)!

String Change Exercise

Play the exercise **tirando**. When changing the strings, prepare the finger on the next string.

The Tirando Stroke
on one String

As the adjacent strings are muted by the alternating rest stroke, when it comes to arpeggios that should sound together, we play them in free stroke (tirando). Now we play the whole piece in free stroke, for the first time also in **tirando alternating stroke** on one string, here the empty G-string, which is the less emphasised middle part!

Andante

Norman Gänser

▶ 97

D.S. = Dal Segno (from the sign) means that you should repeat the piece of music from the sign (bar 9)!

𝄋 = The sign

„al Fine" = (to the end) you therefore play from the sign to "Fine" (bar 16).

Nail Shape and Sound Production

Throughout the history of the guitar there have been many discussions and much controversy about whether one should play with or without the nail. Sounds can either be produced with the fingertip or the fingernails on the "strumming" hand.

Nowadays concert guitarists almost exclusively play the classical guitar with their nails.
Strumming with the nail produces a richer and more nuanced sound.
In addition, the tone is very clear and defined, just as when you play with a plectrum.

Basically, the following applies:

- The nail form conforms to the shape of the fingertip!
- The nail should have no corners and no edges!
- What looks round and smooth will also play round and smooth!

You need:

1. A nail file, that is not too rough, to shape the nails.
   Apparently, a favourite among the nail files is the glass one.
2. A finely gritted file from the chemist or sandpaper from the hardware shop
   (ca. 1000 grit), to smooth the freshly filed, raw nail edge.
3. A file to polish, special micro-mesh polishing cloth,
   or the finest possible sandpaper from the hardware shop.

Filing the Fingernails and the Shape of the Nails:

The string "slides" from the point of contact (1) over the nail and leaves it at the apex (2). The string can swing freely*.

The nail resembles a flattened slope!

Step 1: We also "pull" the nail in this direction over the glass file!
Do not file off too much. You will find the best length on the next page.

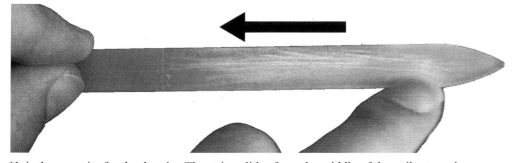

*It is the opposite for the thumbs. The string slides from the middle of the nail outwards.

The Shape of the Nail

Step 2: The fingertip acts as a template for the shape of the nail. It helps if the fingertip and the nail rest on the file at the same time.

Step 3: It is also very important to file the underside of the nail as the string hits the nail from underneath.
Therefore, place the file under the nail and file a sloping surface on the edge of the nail!

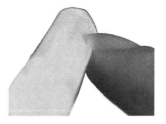

Step 4: Take care that, where the nail and the fingertip come into contact with the string, there are no corners.
The string can often get caught particularly at the beginning of the sloping surface.
File both edges into a rounded shape, both the edge at the beginning of the slope and the edge at the end of the slope!

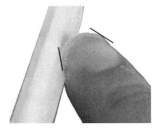

The Length of the Nail

Place your finger on the surface of a table in an angle that is roughly the strumming angle for apoyando. In the ideal case the fingertip and the nail make contact with the surface of the table, whereby a certain resistance is felt by the nail.
If the fingernail does not meet the surface, or the front joint on the fingertip bends too much, then the nail is too short or too long.

OK to too long

Just right

Too short!

Microform and Polishing the Nails

Trimming and Smoothing

When shortening the nails from the underside, the nail edge becomes very thin and sharp.
We can remove this ridge very carefully with some fine sandpaper so that there are no angles.

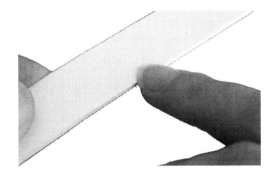

Polishing the Nail Edge

Finally, the nail edge is polished and sealed.
This makes the lovely tone that you hear when professionals play.
Moreover, the nail does not rip so quickly when it is smoothly polished!

Therefore, we polish the nail on the front, the top and above all the underside so that there is a shiny surface on the nail edge.
Almost like glass!

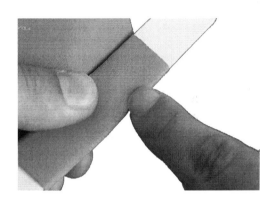

Microform-Tip

Tip!
Before you start rounding off and polishing, try the following:
- Fold the sandpaper once and lay it over the string.
- Hold it in place with your left hand and strum the string wrapped in the paper several times.

This is the way to get rid of any undesirable corners and ridges at exactly the spot where the nail touches the string.
You can also do this with your thumb!

Once you have done this, the nails deserve some grooming!
You can use normal nail or skin oil for this. Simply spread it on the nail bed, the nail edge and the cuticle and let it take effect. This makes the nails more robust.

Le Papillon
Op. 50 Nr. 1

Mauro Giuliani
1781–1829

Scales

Scales are great for both practising one's playing technique and, at the same time, for learning theoretical knowledge and training one's hearing. We can also use them to make the notes on the fingerboard stick in our minds! Play the scales and speak or sing the note names as you do so.

▶100

C-Major Scale in Position II

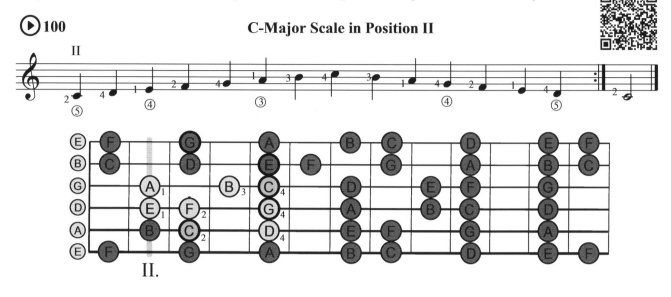

C-Major Scale in Position V

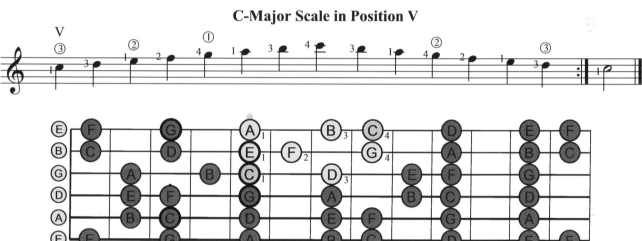

C-Major Scale over two Octaves

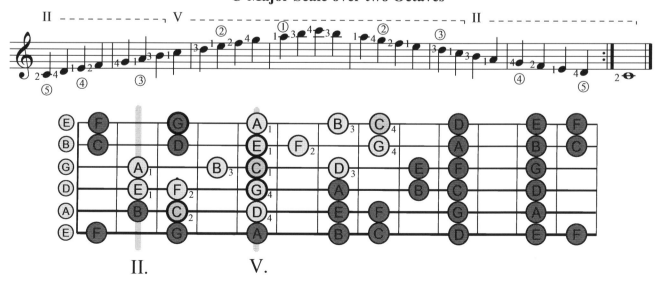

www.guitarschool24.com

Intervals

Intervals are the distances (intervallum, lat. =gap, space) between two notes. They can sound one after the other (successive) or concurrently (simultaneous) as a two-note combination.

The following Latin ordinal numbers are used for the individual notes within a scale and relate to the distance from the root note. From C, E is the third, G is the fifth, etc

First	Second	Third	Fourth	Fifth	Sixth	Seventh	Octave

Intervals between the root note of a major scale and another note on the scale can be "major" or "perfect"!

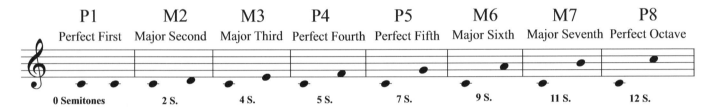

P1	M2	M3	P4	P5	M6	M7	P8
Perfect First	Major Second	Major Third	Perfect Fourth	Perfect Fifth	Major Sixth	Major Seventh	Perfect Octave
0 Semitones	2 S.	4 S.	5 S.	7 S.	9 S.	11 S.	12 S.

Intervals on the fingerboard, starting with the root note P1.

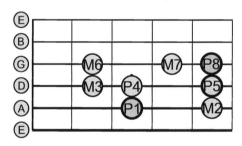

Minor Intervals

m2	m3	m6	m7
Minor Second	Minor Third	Minor Sixth	Minor Seventh

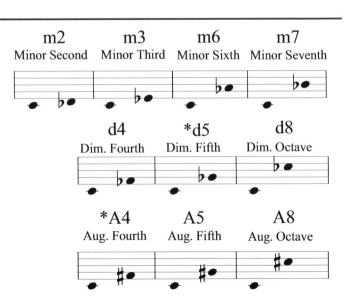

d4	*d5	d8
Dim. Fourth	Dim. Fifth	Dim. Octave

A diminished interval occurs when a perfect (or a minor interval) is reduced (diminished) by one semitone.

*A4	A5	A8
Aug. Fourth	Aug. Fifth	Aug. Octave

An augmented interval occurs when a perfect (or a major interval) is raised by one semitone!

* The so-called **Tritone**

74

Flageolet Tones

Flageolet Tones, or simply flageolets, are a special effect on the guitar.
They sound like high, little bells. In the notes, they can be recognised by diamond-shaped note
heads and the terms arm., ar., or harm.. It is also often indicated over which fret bar
and on which string the flageolet note is to be played.

Lay your ring finger exactly in the **middle** of the string (directly above the 12th fret bar). The finger
only lightly touches the string (do not grip it). As you strum, a vibration node will result, which will
split the string in the middle. Both halves of the string now vibrate separately one **octave** higher.

Immediately after the strum, the gripping finger should be quickly lifted again.
Try also to play the flageolet notes on other strings and on several strings at the same time!

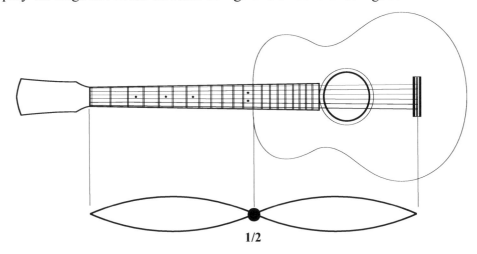

1/2

From a purely physical point of view, **flageolet notes** are overtones. They result from the partial
oscillations of a string. These so-called natural flageolets can also be generated on other places
on the strings.

If one divides the string into **three**, a **fifth** sounds.
Touch the string for this exactly above the 7th fret bar.

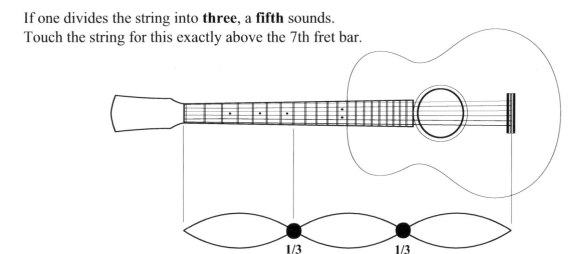

1/3   1/3

If one divides the string into **four**, they sound **two octaves** higher. Grip exactly above the 5th fret bar.

Together with the root note, the first five overtones form a major chord (root note, third, fifth).
The major chord thus occurs naturally! The higher the overtones, the harder they are to create.

For Elise

Arrangement: N.G.

Ludwig van Beethoven
1770-1827

Poco moto

In the guitar notation a diamond-shaped note head is used for the **flageolet** notes, in conjunction with the term harm. (harmonics). Information about the fret bar or/and the strings indicate where they are to be played on the finger board.

Barré Chords

▶ 103

The **Barré** or Bar Chord is executed with the index finger of the gripping hand.
In doing this you press down several strings with one finger.
These chords, that are feared by many, will not be a problem for you,
if your fingers are already accustomed to the movement for these chords,
and the necessary muscles have been trained, by playing and practising them regularly

The following tips (Barré Hacks) will help you do this:

1.) It is better to grip with the **outer edge** of the index finger!
Turn your index finger slightly outwards. The outer edge is actually a little harder.

2.) Grip **very closely** to the fret bar!
Approach: Lay your index finger directly on the fret bar and "roll" it a little outwards.
Well done! You are now pressing close to the fret with the outside edge of your index finger!

3.) Only concentrate on the strings which are **sounding**!
You usually only have to press down a few strings with your index finger!

4.) The **weight of your arm** helps you to press the strings down!
Gravity pulls the elbow down. You hold your hand only with your finger
and with a "light" resistance from the thumb.

4.) The **thumb** is situated in the middle of the back of the guitar neck
  between the index- and middle fingers!

Notation

Half Barré Chord

Full Barré Chord

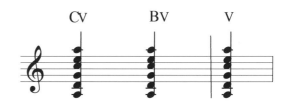

The index finger only presses individual strings!

Barré Chords

Initially the **Barré Chord** poses a challenge for the muscles and joints. Generally, it should be used very deliberately and must be practised. In order to avoid injuries, always practise with breaks and never until your hand is completely exhausted.

It is **never** necessary to grip **all the strings** at the same time.
Usually, it is only individual strings that are pressed with the Barré finger.
The key is the correct weight shifting of the fingers.

▶ **104 Barré-Exercise 1**

Lay your index finger 1 lightly over the 5th fret bar. Play the notes separately and only apply pressure on the notes that are to be played. During the exercise the index finger rolls away on the fret bar.
You will notice that the "middle" strings 4 and 3 are particularly hard to press.
Try to lightly overstretch the Barré finger here.

▶ **105 Barré-Exercise 2**

Here we will practise the Half Barré.
First one string, then two, then three, etc.
You can see the string number which is to be played next to the fret bar number.
Lay your finger therefore only over the strings which are to be played.

Etude in E-Minor

Francisco Tárrega
1852-1909

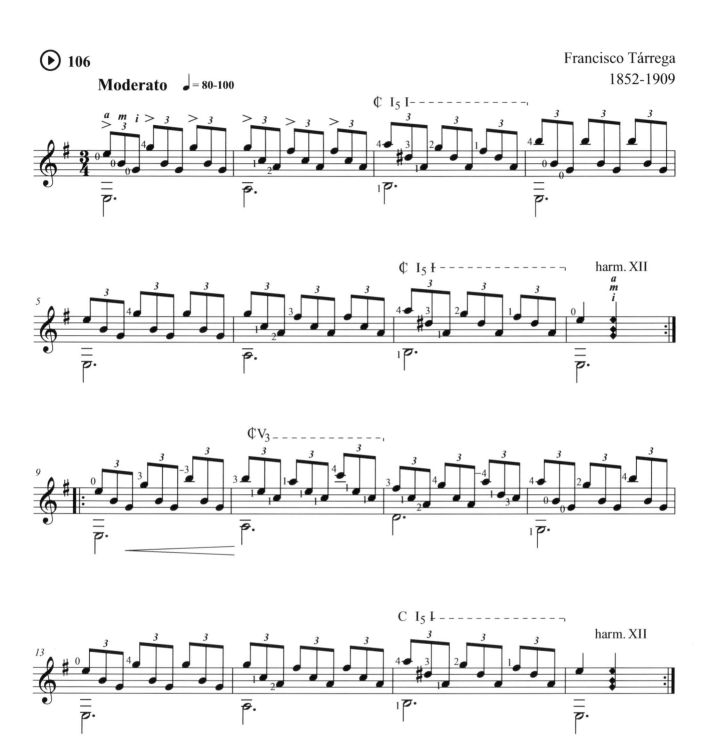

Preparing
"Planting"

▶ 107

The conscious placing of the fingers on the strings before the strumming motion
is called "preparing" (or, in English, **"planting"**).

Preparatory Exercises are very effective exercises for the plucking hand.
They contribute greatly to stability, reflex development, and accuracy.

1.) Staccato Planting

Place your finger again in the basic position on the strings (as described in Book 2, Page 1).
Play the strings and stop them immediately afterwards by laying your finger back on the strings again.
Then play the next note when all your fingers are back on the strings again
This exercise should be played at a slow tempo, but with the fingers moving relatively quickly.
Try to "feel" the contact point.

2.) Block-Planting

Here all fingers are prepared simultaneously. Start again in the basic position and remove your fingers
one by one from the strings with the strum. When p plays again, place all fingers at the same time
on the strings.

3.) Sequential Planting

Each finger is prepared separately (sequentially). While thumb p plays, place index finger i on the string
at the same time. While index finger i plays, place your middle finger on simultaneously, etc.
Thus, one finger is always lying on a string. Keep your hand still, only the fingers play.

Chord Steps and Functions

▶ 108

If one builds **triads** above every note on the major scale with the notes in the respective key, the result will be main and subordinate triads (chords). They are built on a root note and are layered in so-called **thirds**, as in the "snowman principle".
Thirds can be **major** (4 semitones) or **minor** (3 semitones).
The scale's major and minor chords come from the layering of these thirds

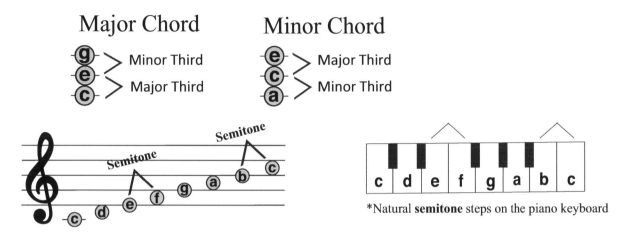

*Natural **semitone** steps on the piano keyboard

Every triad in a scale fulfils a function whereby we can generate tension and relaxation in the music!
The most important functions in music are:
Scale Degree 1 (**Tonic**), Scale Degree IV (**Subdominant**) and Scale Degree V (**Dominant**).
Example C-Major Scale:

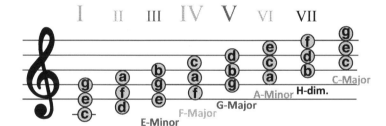

The other chords serve as "chord substitutions" for the three main chords. Work them in as well!
Scale Degree IV (Tonic Parallel), Scale Degree II (Subdominant Parallel),
Scale Degree III (Dominant Parallel or Tonic Counter Parallel).

The Cadence

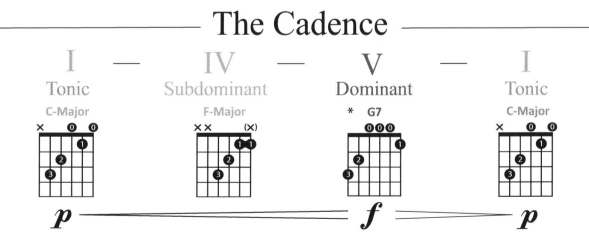

* On the dominant scale degree, a dominant seventh chord (7) is often played to emphasise the tension!

Caprice

„Allegro" Op. 30 Nr.13

Mauro Giuliani
1781–1829

Scales

⏵ 110

The following major scales over two octaves are particularly suited for you to explore the finger board.
Simply shift the grip example for the scale from the root note on the fret bar VII (C) to fret bar II and
play the G-Major scale from G! The G-Major scale has a # accidental, namely F sharp.
You can move the major scales to any desired root note.

Use these scales as well to imprint the notes on the finger board!
Play the scales and speak or sing the note names as you do so.

C-Major Scale in Position VII

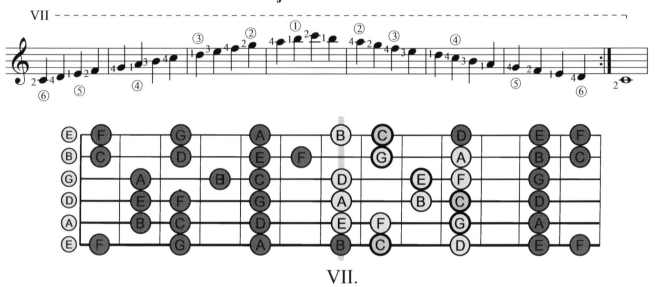

G-Major Scale in Position II

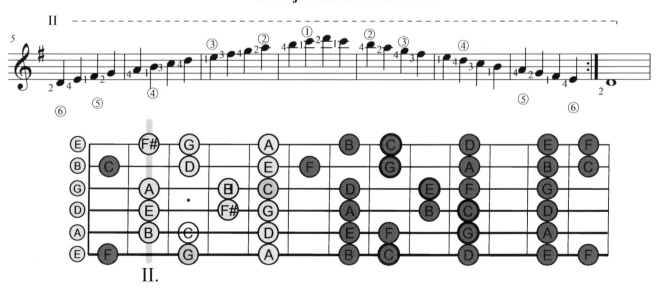

Note Quiz

111 Enter the names of the notes on the finger board and write them on the stave.

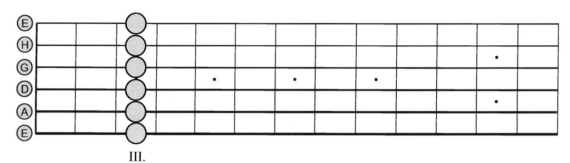

III.

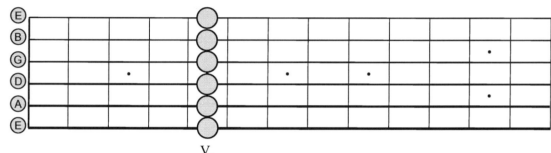

V.

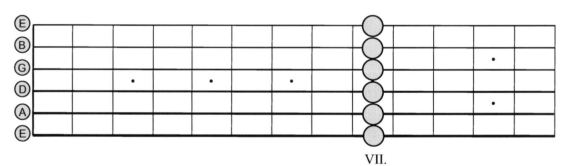

VII.

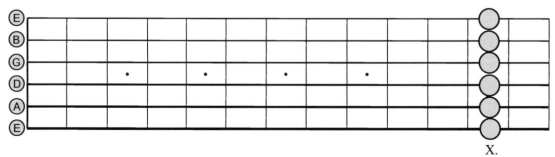

X.

Lagrima
(Preludio)

Francisco Tárrega
1852-1909

▶ 112

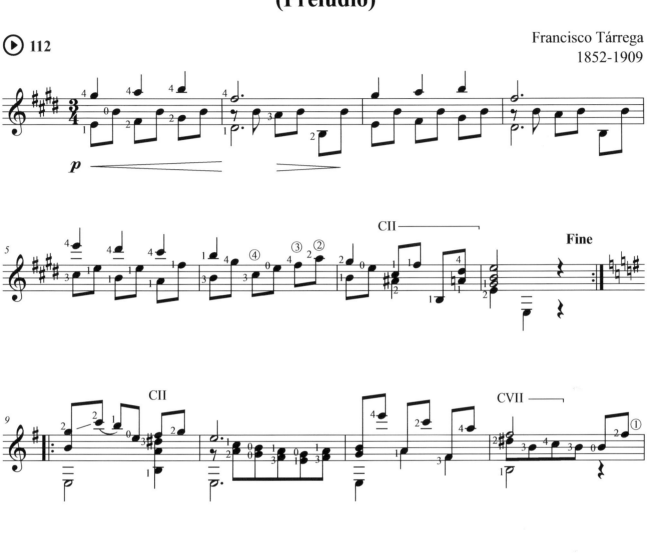

CII — Fine

CII CVII — D.C. al Fine

p

© Norman Gänser
www.guitarschool24.com

85

Circle of Fifths

The **Circle of Fifths** is a tool often used to illustrate the scales and how they are related.
It resembles the face of a clock, whereby the **major scales** can be found on the outside
and the **minor scales** on the inside.

Scales whose root notes are a **perfect fifth** apart are closely related, for example, C-Major and G-Major.
Two scales are "parallel" if they have the same accidentals, for example, C-Major and A-Minor.

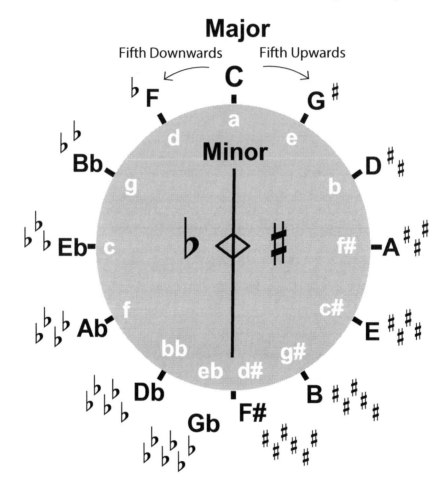

♯ **Good Days Always End By F♯eeling C♯heerful**
♭ **Feel B♭better E♭ven A♭fter D♭ays G♭o C♭razy**

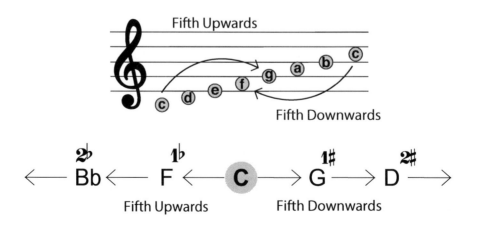

Scale Exercise

A Reminder:

(▶) 114

The C-Major scale has no accidentals!

Every major scale consists of two semitone steps (between the 3rd and 4th,
and likewise between the 7th and the 8th degree of the scale) and five whole note steps!

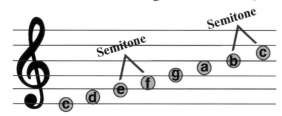

Complete the scales, draw in the semitone steps, and write the note names below them!

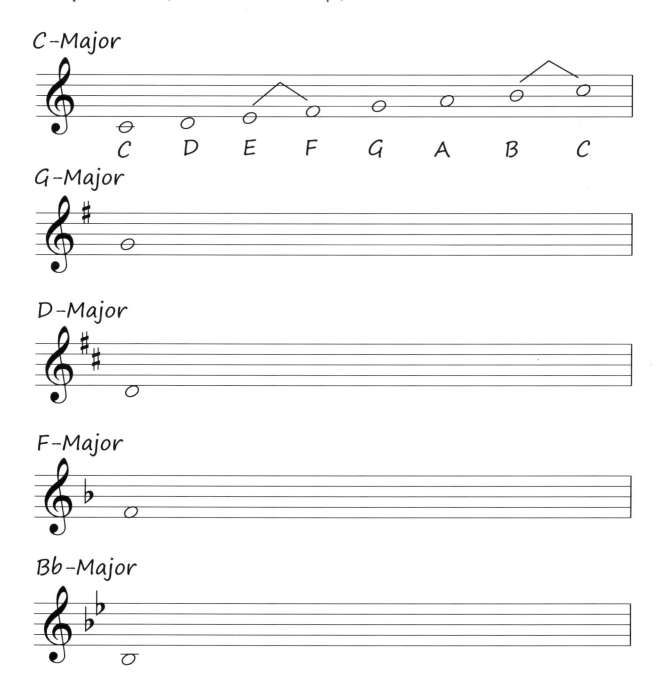

C-Major

C   D   E   F   G   A   B   C

G-Major

D-Major

F-Major

Bb-Major

Spanish Romance

Traditional Spanish Song

Anonymous

Practice Tips

With the following tips you can achieve the best conditions for successful practising.
Practice means: *Time for YOU!*

First: The Correct Time Management

Enter your practice times in a calendar and/or your smartphone or write them down on a piece of paper. Everyone learns at a different pace: some learn best during the day and others learn best in the evening. Try to keep to fixed practice times and lengths.
Practising should become a matter of course.

Second: The appropriate environment

Take a quick moment to set up the area in which you will practise. You should feel comfortable there and, if possible, you should be undisturbed for the desired duration. Take everything that you will need with you – your guitar, your tuning device, the music, the metronome, a pencil – and avoid distractions. You will not be able to concentrate on practising in a noisy place.

Third: Define tasks and goals

Your learning goals should be defined before you practise. Set yourself small, reachable goals before practising. You can write them down in a notebook or on the sheet of music. After practising make a note of what you have achieved. If you do not achieve your learning goals in this practice session, you will reach them in the next one. In this way you can track your progress and stay focused and motivated.

Fourth: Concentration

Practise slowly and with concentration. Important: Your brain of course also notices the mistakes that you make, and they can become a habit. If you play a passage incorrectly, take the time to make yourself aware of the problem. Are you playing too fast? Are you holding your fingers or your thumbs in the wrong way? Try to practise only this part with the mistake again and again, if necessary, very slowly and, if possible, without mistakes so that you can improve.

Fifth: Relax and prepare your mind

Only those who can really relax can also concentrate well. You can achieve this by the correct "mental preparation". Sit down on your chair and make yourself aware that you are sitting there at this moment. Take a deep breath and feel your own weight on the chair. Breathe deeply one more time and look forward to your well-earned practice session. Concert guitarists use this "preparation" method on, for example, the stage in front of an audience.

Practice Plan

Following a **Practice Plan** is however a proven method for goal-oriented and efficient practising. Every person is different and needs his own tailor-made practice plan. It is the length of the practice session which varies above all and this depends ultimately on your own goals and expectations.

Therefore, you should know beforehand what you are aiming for (what is your goal?) and why do you want to it (what is your motivation?). Why do you want to reach this goal? What will change for you personally if you reach it? Your Practice Plan is therefore guided by your goals and by how much you are prepared to invest in reaching your goals?

An example of a Practice Plan could look like this:

PRACTICE PLAN

Warming Up

5 minutes left hand (preliminary exercise)

5 minutes technical drill (exercises)

Block 1

5 minutes problem area piece 1

10 minutes play through piece 1

Break 15 minutes (Stretching)

Block 2

5 minutes new piece

20 minutes finishing up (playing whatever you feel like)

PRACTICE PLAN

Guitar Practice Session Template

Practising the guitar is a science in itself! There is so much that you have to watch out for at the same time. Set just one "practice goal" for yourself every day and write it down!

Write down what you are going to work on that day. Are you pressing too hard, too inaccurately? Is your body relaxed?

I would like to give you a tool that has helped me practise more consciously. The Practice Triangle. Try again and again while you are practising to think of the three corners and, if necessary, to make corrections. In the middle there are the three key parameters of music.

Body: correct, relaxed posture of the body and the guitar
Left Hand: precise grip close to the fret bars but not pressing too hard
Right Hand: good tone and legato

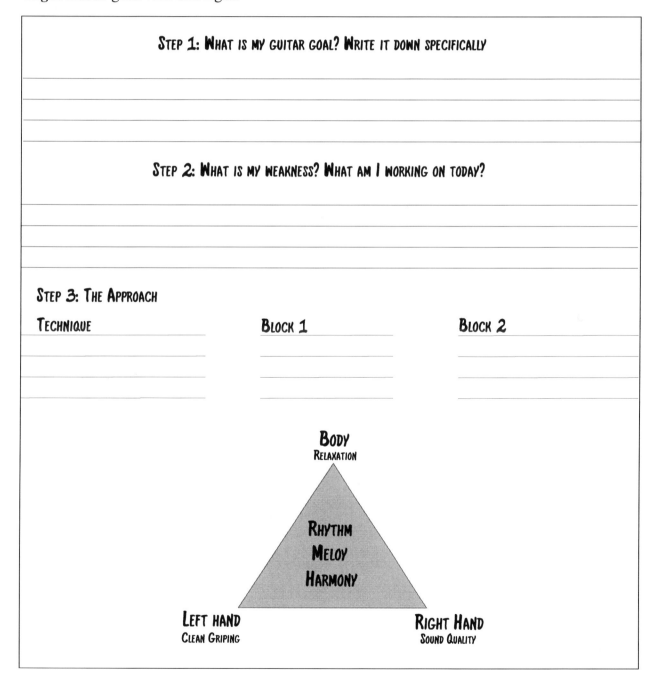

STEP 1: WHAT IS MY GUITAR GOAL? WRITE IT DOWN SPECIFICALLY

STEP 2: WHAT IS MY WEAKNESS? WHAT AM I WORKING ON TODAY?

STEP 3: THE APPROACH

TECHNIQUE   BLOCK 1   BLOCK 2

BODY
RELAXATION

RHYTHM
MELOY
HARMONY

LEFT HAND
CLEAN GRIPING

RIGHT HAND
SOUND QUALITY

Flamenco
Guitar Course

Course Introduction

An excellent introduction to the world of flamenco guitar is the **Soleares** style, also called Soleá. This is one of the fundamental flamenco styles, which combines both the typical flamenco **rhythm** and the most common **tonality**.

In addition, the most important **techniques** of the flamenco guitar can be demonstrated and explained on the basis of the Soleá. That's why the **lessons** of this course will be about this and I would like to give a few explanations verbally in advance.

Rhythm: Many flamenco rhythms are based on a scheme with twelve beats, which provides for certain accentuations.

In **Soleá** it looks like this: 1 2 **3** 4 5 **6** 7 **8** 9 **10** 11 **12** (the bold numbers symbolize the accents).
This rhythmic structure has to be represented with the help of the different techniques and with the corresponding harmonic changes.

You can also get an overview of this topic with the help of the **Reloj del Flamenco** (Flamenco Clock). The **Compás** is the basic rhythm, which consists of twelve beats with a fixed emphasis!

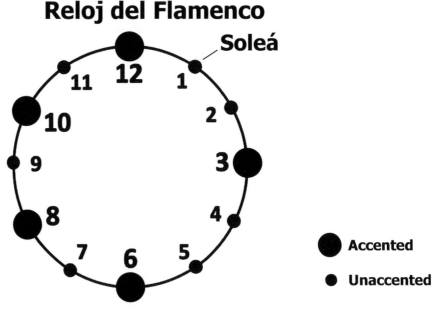

Key: The Soleá moves in the **Phrygian key**, which begins on the third degree of the normal major scale (which is actually the Ionian scale). In the concrete case, this means that the beginning and the end of the scale of our Soleá is the E, using the tonal material of C major (E F G A H C D E).

In most cases, we also add the G sharp from the harmonic A minor scale parallel to C major.
The harmonies used are the familiar flamenco cadence: A minor, G major, F major and E major.

Flamenco Techniques

On the one hand, the **flamenco guitar** uses various playing techniques that differ only slightly from those of the **classical guitar** (e.g. arpeggios, alternating strokes).

On the other hand, there are also techniques that are used in this form almost only on the flamenco guitar, e.g. rasgueados, special techniques of thumb strumming and tapping on the guitar top.
You will learn the following techniques in this course:

Rasgueado: A rasgueado is generally understood to be the striking of several strings in rapid succession with different fingers, whether in sixteenth, in triplet or sixth stolenfigures.

Pulgar: The thumb stroke is almost always applied (apoyando) on the flamenco guitar, in all contexts.

Picado: Single-line scale passages performed by playing alternately with the index and middle fingers, supporting the other fingers on the string immediately above (Apoyando).

Golpe: Tapping on the guitar top (in Spanish "golpe") is often used to emphasize some notes or to mark certain accents. Sometimes it is simply used in a very flexible way to play syncopated with the rhythm. The taps ("golpes") are executed mainly with the nail of the ringfinger on the guitar top below the strings. In rarer cases, the Zeigefinger is also used in conjunction with a powerful downstroke with a tap above the strings.

Tremolo: The most common tremolo in flamenco today is: piami. It is notated as a quintole, but is generally played in a more rhythmically free (expressive) manner. For example, sometimes a small delay may be appropriate between the bass and the first index finger.

We will cover all these topics in this course, with the goal that at the end you will be able to play a small piece of an authentic Soleá on the guitar.

**I hope you will have fun entering the fascinating world of flamenco.
I wish you much success with it!**

Andreas Maria Germek
and Norman Gänser

Conotations

All fingeringsand indications
confirm with international standards.
Following Explanations may be useful:

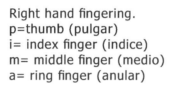

Right hand fingering.
p=thumb (pulgar)
i= index finger (indice)
m= middle finger (medio)
a= ring finger (anular)

Left hand fingering.
1= index finger
2= middle finger
3= ring finger
4= little finger

Golpe: Hit the guitar top with your nail.
Mostly done with the ring finger a. Don`t
hit without protection
above the wood (Golpeador).

Downstroke
from the low to the high E string.

Upstroke
from the high to the low E string.

Lesson 1
Soleá Rasgueado

The **Soleá** (also called Soleares) is counted on 12 beats, whereby the beats 3, 6, 8, 10 and 12 are accented. The **Rasgueado** arrangement chosen here is a very common way to play this rhythm on the guitar. The small box above the respective note means that together with this stroke a **Golpe** (tap) is performed with the ring finger (a) on the guitar top.

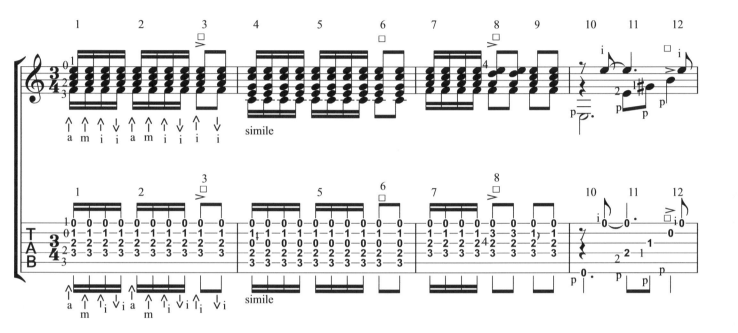

In the following, this **Rasgueado** is melodically varied a little by leaving the little finger of the left hand on the g (3rd fret) of the high E1-string until the eighth count

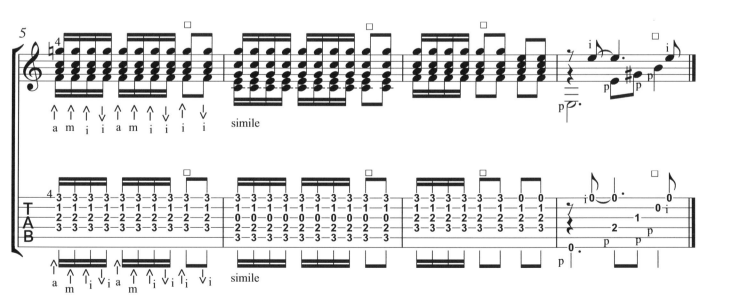

Lesson 2
Soleá Falseta, Pulgar (thumb)

In flamenco, a **falseta** is a small guitar melody or variation that allows the flamenco guitar to play a melodic solo role based on the respective compás (as opposed to the usual accompaniment function for singing or dancing).
Our falseta here is played in an alternating pattern between thumb and index finger.
Please pay attention to even semiquavers and to the technical execution of the thumb attack seen in the video.

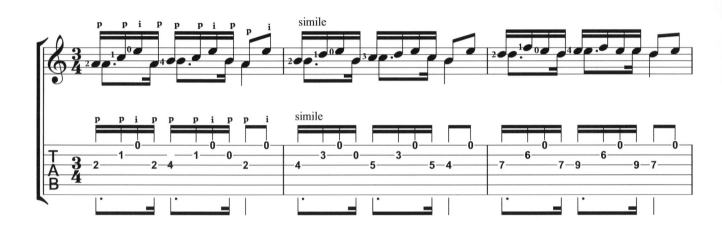

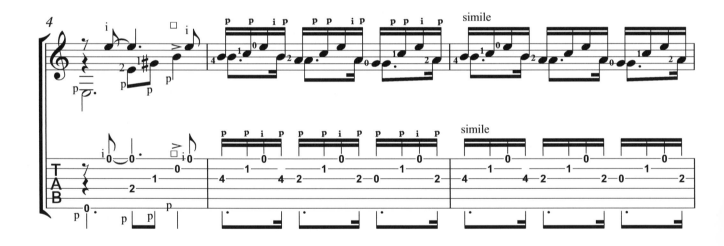

Lesson 3
Soleá Falseta, Arpeggio

The following is a very typical falseta for the **Soleá**, based on a thumb melody combined with an accompanying **arpeggio**. Please remember that also in the arpeggio the thumb is always played apoyando (applied) as long as it does not thereby block the adjacent string).

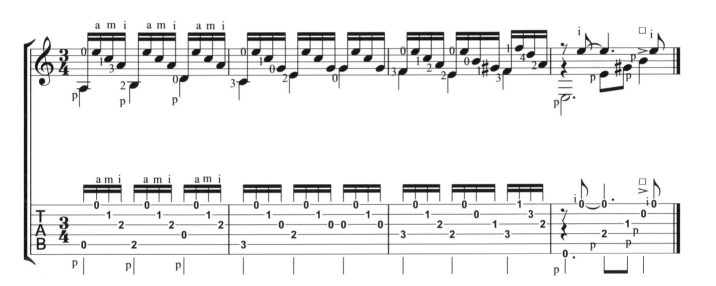

Lesson 4
Filling compas Soleá and variation

This way of creating the Soleá 12 rhythm is often used in song or dance accompaniment, but also in solo playing. With the help of different variations, it's a discreet way to keep the rhythm going.

The following is a small variation: the first beats are executed as above, and from the seventh beat a short **Picado** (scale in alternating beat) leads up to the ten and thus to the final remate.

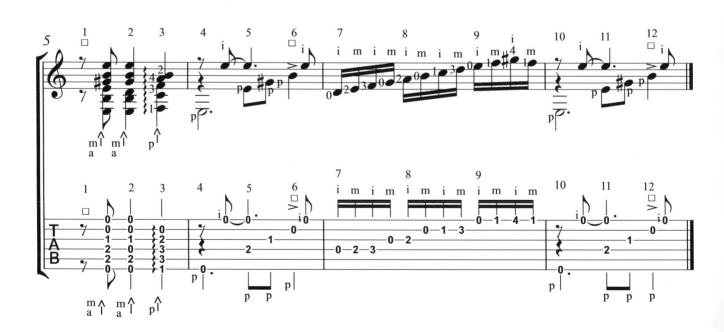

Lesson 5
Soleá Chord Variation/Intro

This lesson is about tapping (**Golpe**) to finish the rasgueado. The corresponding symbols for this (small box above the staff) were already entered in the first lesson (see there).

New material here is a small chord variation that can be used both in between, but especially as an intro or at the end of a soleá. In principle, a **Golpe** can be made on each of the following thumb taps, but this is not required, so I have not notated the Golpes.
It is important, however, to keep the pause after the tenth count and to end the compás with a golpe on the twelfth.

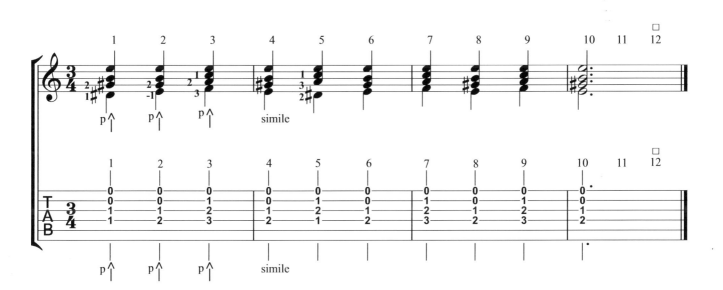

Bonus Lesson
Soleá Falseta, Tremolo

Tremolo is a specialty on the flamenco guitar. By striking a string quickly and repeatedly, it creates the illusion of a sustained, continuous tone. The tremolo technique in flamenco differs from the classical tremolo by an additional stroke. The finger sequence of thumb (p), index finger (i), ring finger (a), middle finger (m) and again index finger (i) results in quintuplets. Please remember that also in tremolo the thumb is played apoyando (applied), as long as it does not block the adjacent string.

© Norman Gänser
www.guitarschool24.com

About the Flamenco Guitar

Flamenco music and dance in its current form is a relatively young art.
It is believed that the unity of the three flamenco elements (song, dance, guitar) was consolidated only in the course of the nineteenth century.

Before that, flamenco was represented mainly by singing (canté) and flamenco dance (baile). The guitar (toque) gained importance relatively late and also only as an accompanying instrument.

Since the first flamenco guitarists were probably not too great virtuosos, it can be assumed that they were looking for the simplest but most effective means possible to accompany the singing on the guitar.

This explains the frequent use of "open" chords in the traditional form of flamenco styles. The accompaniment was mainly created with rasgueados, and the sparse independent melodies were played mainly with the thumb.

Flamenco guitar is usually considered to be very difficult to play. But in fact there is also an "easy approach". If you think about the history, you will realize that flamenco music was actually made for the guitar and therefore, unlike some classical music, it is especially adapted to the conditions of the guitar.

It was only when flamenco left its original family and rather private framework and began to assert itself as an attractive stage art (from about the second half of the 19th century) that all three elements of flamenco gained more and more artistry and virtuosity.
This also affected the guitar, and it is from this period that the first names of guitarists, some of them already quite virtuosic and artistically demanding, have been handed down (e.g. Miguel Barrull, Manolo de Huelva).

The first flamenco guitarist who could make a name for himself as a soloist with independent flamenco compositions was Ramon Montoya, also basically an accompanist of great singers (e.g. Antonio Chacon) and female singers (e.g. "La Nina de los Peines").

He was followed by numerous virtuosos of the flamenco guitar and great musicians, such as Nino Ricardo, Sabicas, Paco de Lucia and many others of the current younger generation.
It should be mentioned that all these outstanding soloists have always been and still are great accompanists of the singing. Because: In order to understand flamenco and to be able to perform it adequately as a soloist on the guitar, there is ultimately no way around singing and dancing.

Parallel to the studies it is therefore very helpful to listen to flamenco (especially in its "traditional" form). Solo guitar and styles with vocals.

The difference between
Classical Guitar and Flamenco Guitar

At first glance, the flamenco guitar differs from the classical concert guitar only by its pickguard, the **golpeador**.

But there are mainly structural differences, which are rooted in the different use of the instruments.

In the beginning, the flamenco guitar (guitarra flamenca) was almost exclusively an accompanying instrument for flamenco singing (canté) and flamenco dancing (baile). Compared to the loud percussive footwork of the flamenco dancers and the powerful vocals of the flamenco singers, the flamenco guitars were always relatively quiet.

The flamenco guitarist had difficulty presenting the guitar sounds audibly.
So the requirement for the guitar makers (the guitarrero) was to build a louder, more assertive instrument. The foundation for the creation of the flamenco guitar was laid.

The flamenco guitar reacts very quickly, the sound is loud, percussive and crisp, but does not stay as long as that of a pure concert guitar. The main reasons for this are the thinner walls and the lower string action.

Constructional differences:
 A proper flamenco guitar should have a striker guard (golpeador) on the top. This is a transparent or white, hard plastic film that protects the soundboard from the blows (golpes) that are made on the soundboard in many flamenco pieces to emphasize the beat (compás).

Please pay attention if you play the course with a classical guitar.

The string action of the flamenco guitar is lower than that of classical guitars. This makes the guitar easier to play. However, the vibrating string also hits the frets more easily when played more forcefully. This creates a buzzing sound that is not very desirable, especially for solo and concert guitarists (and spectators).

Therefore, on more modern instruments, the strings are not as low as on older flamenco guitars, which were primarily used as accompaniment instruments. The distance between the strings and the top and fingerboard of a guitar can be changed or adjusted. Such work should only be done by a professional.
The flamenco guitar is lighter than the concert guitar. The thickness of the wood used for the top, back and sides is thinner than that of a normal classical guitar. In addition, the body of the flamenco guitar is not as deep as that of its classical sister. The sides are on average about 2 cm narrower.
There are two types of flamenco guitars, which differ in the wood used:

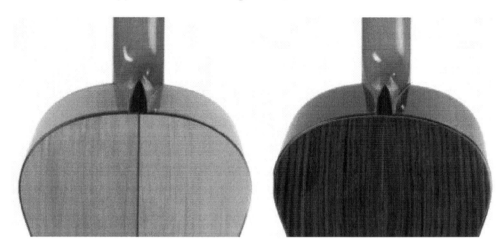

Flamenca Blanca

A "blanca" is traditionally a guitar with back and sides made of light (blanca) cypress wood (rarely maple). These guitars have the typical clear, percussive and crisp flamenco sound. However, the reverberation time of the tones is much less than that of "normal" concert guitars.

The Blancas are predestined for dance and vocal accompaniment due to their volume and assertiveness.

Flamenca Negra

Negra" refers to instruments with dark (negro) wood, predominantly "rosewood" is used. A Flamenca Negra is generally more similar to a concert guitar. It has a slightly broader sound than the Blanca, has more reverberation time and is therefore more suitable as a concert and solo instrument.

Other styles can also be played with a Negra without any problems. This makes it the perfect choice for the more versatile guitarist.

Technique and interpretation compared with the classical guitar

Apart from some special playing techniques, the flamenco guitar technique does not differ too much from the one used on the classical guitar.

A slightly different handling results, however, from the sound ideal and the musical design prevailing in flamenco: the tone is generally rather "pointed", clear and concise, which means that the striking hand moves mainly between the bridge and the sound hole, standing more or less perpendicular to the strings.

Thumb techniques (Pulgar): The thumb attack is played almost exclusively applied (apoyando). This is true not only where it takes on melodic function, but also in places where it plays the bass to arpeggios and tremolos.

Picado: The same applies to runs ("picados"), which are also almost always played apoyando. Golpe (tapping): This involves tapping the top of the guitar for the purpose of accentuation or rhythmic support while playing. This is done either with the nail of the ring finger under the strings or with the nail of the index finger above the strings (for strong chords). Rasgueado: In principle it concerns with the

Rasgueado is a usually quite fast, successive striking of several strings with one or different fingers. Rasgueados almost always have a clear rhythmic structure, e.g. sixteenths, eighth or sixteenth triplets, quintuplets, etc.. In order to achieve a good flamenco sound, it is especially important that the individual fingers strike the strings in quick, independent movements and do not "scrape" over the remaining strings while lying on one string.

Alzapua: This is a "speciality" in which the thumb strikes several or individual strings alternately in a rapid up and down movement, thus producing a strongly rhythmic bass melody with simultaneous chord accompaniment.

Tremolo: The tremolo in flamenco has one beat more than the classical tremolo (piami vs. pami). It is therefore a little denser and does not have to be played so evenly. For example, sometimes a small delay may be appropriate between the bass and the first index finger. In more modern flamenco, other tremolo techniques are also used, for example with the following formula: (pa)miami, notated as sextole (thumb and first ring finger are struck together).

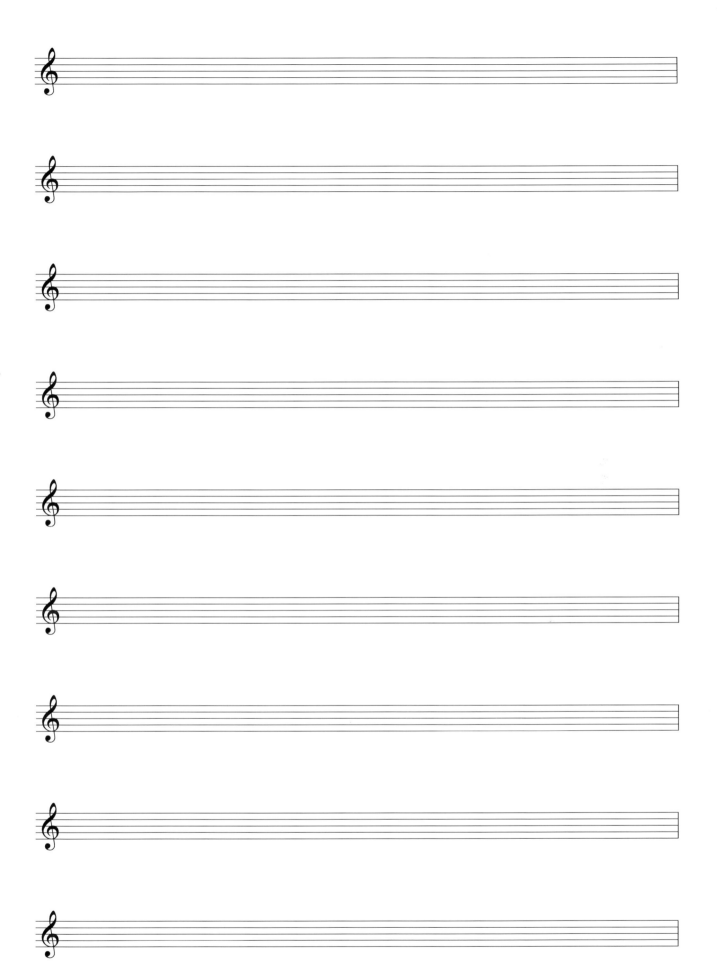

Made in the USA
Las Vegas, NV
22 February 2024

86106843R00059